Workshop Technology-III

Workshop Technology-I

[illegible]

[illegible]

Published [illegible]
An ISO 9001:2008 [illegible]
VAYU EDUCATION [illegible]
2/25, Ansari Road, Darya Ganj, [illegible]
Ph: 91-11-47236600, [illegible]
Fax: 91-11-41564440
[illegible]

Workshop Technology-III

PROF. (DR.) K.S. YADAV

Professionally U.K. Trained Educationist and Writer

Director

Satyam College of Engineering and Management, Delhi-NCR

International Institute of Technology and Management (IITM), Murthal, Sonepat

Formerly Director

Subharti Institute of Technology and Engineering, Meerut,

Shri Balwant Institute of Technology, Sonepat,

South Point College of Engineering and Management, Sonepat,

ABSS Institute of Technology, Meerut,

Aravali College of Engineering and Management, Faridabad

AN ISO 9001:2008 CERTIFIED COMPANY

Vayu Education of India

2/25, Ansari Road, Darya Ganj, New Delhi-110 002

Workshop Technology-III

ISBN: 978-93-80712-54-3

First Edition: 2013

Price: ₹ 120.00

Printed & bound in India

Published by:

AN ISO 9001:2008 CERTIFIED COMPANY

VAYU EDUCATION OF INDIA

2/25, Ansari Road, Darya Ganj, New Delhi-110 002

Ph.: 91-11-47236600, 41564445

Fax: 91-11-41564440

E-mail: vei@veiindia.com

Web: www.veiindia.com

Preface

A Strong need has been felt for a good book on WORKSHOP TECHNOLOGY-III for use of engineering students. This book has been attempted with this sole purpose in mind. The book provides a great deal of information in a comprehensive style on various aspects of Workshop Technology. The object of this book is to present the subject-matter in a most concise, compact, to the point and lucid manner.

While writing the book, I have constantly kept in mind the various requirements of the students. No effort has been spared to enrich the book with simple language and self explanatory diagrams. Every care has been taken not to make the book voluminous, as the students have also to face other subjects of equal importance.

Keeping in view the readership of this book, every effort has been made to present the subject-matter in a simple language and style. Various steps for producing an object have been outlined to lend clarity to various manufacturing processes. In short, it is hoped that the book will embrace the requirements of all the engineering processes, and will earn appreciation of all the fellow teachers.

This book on Workshop Technology-III has been written specially to cater the needs of second year students of Mechanical Engineering. It covers comprehensively the latest syllabus as prescribed by State Board of Technical Education, Haryana, M.D. University, Rohtak and other Universities and Egineering Colleges. It covers the topics of Modern Machining Processes, Plastic Moulding Techniques, Metallic Coating Processes, Gear Manufacturing, Finishing Processes and Jigs and Fixtures.

I am grateful to Mr. Ankur Sachdeva, Deptt. of Mech. Engg., Northern India Engg. College (N.I.E.C.), Delhi. Affiliated to G.G.S.I.P. University, Delhi for his assistance and useful suggestions.

Although every care has been taken to check the mistakes and misprints, yet it is difficult to claim perfection. Errors, omissions and suggestions for the improvement of this volume, will thankfully be acknowledged and incorporated in the next edition.

I am grateful to my publisher, Vayu Education of India, New Delhi, Dr. R.K. Jain for his initiative efforts and determination to bring out this book in the shortest possible time.

New Delhi, **DR. K.S. YADAV**

Content

Chapter 1

Modern Machining Processes

1.1 INTRODUCTION

From some time past, engineering industries have witnessed a rapid growth in the development of harder and difficult to machine materials such as corhides, stainless steel, heat resisting steels, tungsten and many other high strength-temperature resistant (HSTR) alloys. These materials find wide applications in aerospace, nuclear, engineering and other industries owing to their high strength-to-weight ratio, hardness and heat resisting qualities. For such materials the conventional edged tool machining, inspite of recent technological advancement, is highly uneconomical and the degree of accuracy and surface finish attainable are poor. Machining of these materials into complex shape is difficult, time consuming and sometimes impossible.

In view of the seriousness of the problem, Merchant (1960) emphasized the need for the development of newer concepts in metal machining. By adopting a unified programme and utilizing the results of basic and applied research, it has now become possible to process some of the materials which were formerly considered to be unmachinable under normal conditions. The newer, machining processes, so developed, are often called MODERN MACHINING PROCESSES of Unconventional Machining Methods. These are unconventional in the sense that they do not employ a conventional or traditional tool for metal removal, insted, they directly utilize some form of energy for metal machining.

1.1.1 Classification

Newer machining methods can be classified on the basic of the type of energy they employ for the purpose of metal removal. Broadly speaking they car be classified as below:

1. Mechanical Metal Removal Processes.
2. Electro-chemical Metal Removal Processes.
3. Thermal Metal Removal Processes.

1.2 MECHANICAL PROCESSES

Mechanical methods are characterised by the fact that material removal is due to the application of mechanical energy in the form of high frequency vibrations or kinetic energy of abrasive jet. Practical

Machining methods that employ mechanical energy are: (*i*) Ultra-sonic Machining (USM), (*ii*) Abrasive Jet Machining (AJM), and (iii) Water Jet Machining (WJM).

1.3 ULTRASONIC MACHINING (USM)

The term ultrasonics is used to describe vibrationals waves having a frequency above the hearing range of normal human ear *i.e.*, beyond 18 KHz. In USM (also known as Ultra-sonic Grinding or Impact Grinding) material is removed due to action of abrasive grains which are hammered into the work surface by a tool oscillating at a high frequency normal to the work surface. For this purpose, a tool oscillation frequency, in the range of 20 KHz to 30 KHz and an amplitude of about 0.2mm have been found to be appropriate. Ultrasonics are generated by feeding the high frequency electrical current to a transdercer which it to high frequency mechanical vibrations. The vibrations thus produced are focussed to the cutting point by means of horn. Abrasive for use in this process is supplied in the form of slurry suspended in a carrier fluid, and the tool feed is achieved by means of static loading of vibrator head. USM is a copying operation where the shape produced is mirror image of the tool. Thus accuracy of machining in this case depends upon manufacturing accuracy of the tool itself (dimensional accuracy upto ± 0.005mm is possible). Range of sizes of USM machines varies from 20W to 2KW.

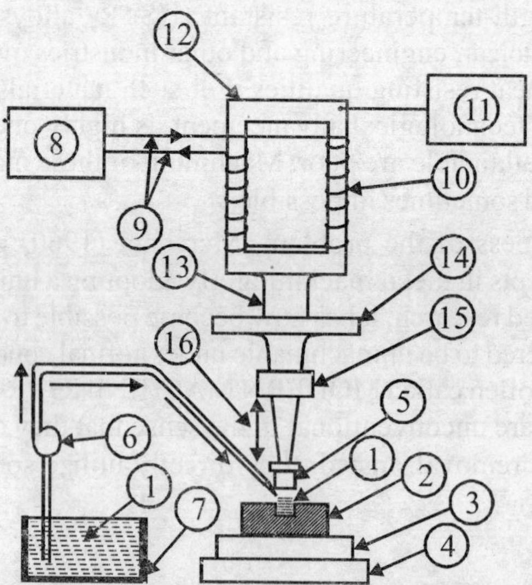

Fig. 1.1: Principle of Ultrasonic Machining 1. Abrasive slurry, 2. Workpiece, 3. Fixture, 4. Table, 5. Cutting tool, 6. Circulating pump, 7. Reservoir, 8. Ultrasonic oscillator, 9. Leads, 10. Excitation coil, 11. Feed mechanism, 12. Ultrasonic transducer, 13. Transducer cone or horn, 14. Connecting body, 15. Tool holder, 16. Direction of tool motion.

1.3.1 Elements of the Process

The important elements of the ultra-sonic process are:

(*i*) Generator (*ii*) Transducer, (*iii*) Abrasives, (*iv*) Work Material and (*v*) Tool Shape and Material.

(*i*) Generators: The electronic oscillator and amplifier are known as GENERATOR, which converts the available electrical energy of low frequency to high frequency power of the order of 20 KHz which is supplied to the transducer.

(*ii*) Transducer: The device for converting any type of energy into ultrasonic waves is ULTRASONIC TRANSDUCER. The electrical energy can be converted into mechanical vibrations by magne-trostriction effect exhibited by some metals. Magne-trostriction means a change in dimension occuring in ferromagnetic materials subject to an alternating magnetic field. The high frequency power supplied by the ultrasonic oscillator to the ultrasonic transducer activates the stock of the magne-trostrictive material which produces longitudinal vibratory motion of the tool. The amplitude of the vibration is inadequate for cutting purpose. This is therefore, transmitted to the penetrating tool through mechanical focussing device, which provides an intense vibration of the desired amplitude at the tool end. The mechanical focussing device is some times called a Velocity Transformer. This is vertually a tapered shank (HORN), its upper end being rigidly clamped or brazed to the lower face of the magne-trostrictive material (NICKEL), and its lower end is provided with means for securing the tool. All these parts including the cutting tool act as one elastic body transmitting vibrations to the TIP of the CUTTING TOOL.

(*iii*) Abrasives: The commonly used abrasives are Aluminium oxide (Al_2O_3), Boron carbide (B_4C), Silicon Carbide (SiC) and Diamond dust. Boron carbide is most expensive abrasive material and best suited to cutting of tungsten carbide, tool steel and precious stones. Silicon carbide is a general purpose abrasive applicable to a variety of situations. For cutting glass and ceramics, Alumina is found as the best. The abrasive slurry is circulated to the work-tool interface by a CIRCULATING PUMP. A refrigerated cooling system is used to cool the abrasive slurry to a temperature of 5° to 6°C. A good method is to keep the slurry in a bath in cutting zone. The size of abrasive varies between 200 to 2000 grit. Coarse grades are good for ROUGHING, whereas finer grades, say 1000 grits are used for finishing. Fresh abrasives cut better and the slurry therefore be replaced periodically. For use of ultrasonic machines the abrasive is suspended in a liquid media. Water satisfies most of the requirements and hence is used often. In order to prevent rusting some anti-corrosive inhibitors are added. As the tool vibrates with a specific frequency, an abrasive slurry, usually a mixture of abrasive grains and water of definite proportion (20–30 per cent) is made to flow under pressure through the tool-work piece interface. The impact force arising out of the vibration of the tool end and the flow of slurry through the work-tool interface actually causes thousands of microscopic grains to remove the work material by abrasion. The tool has the some shape as the cavity to be machined.

(*iv*) Work Material: The method of USM is chiefly employed to machine hard and brittle materials like carbides, glass, ceramics, silicon, precious stones, germanium, titanium, tungsten, tool steels, die steels and ferrite quartz etc. The vibrating frequency per second such a high frequency, which is more than the upper limit of audible frequency for human ear, makes the process inaudible (silent). An Electro-mechanical Transducer is used for producing this high frequency of vibrations.

(*v*) **Tool Shape and Material:** The tool shape has an important effect on the rate of tool penetration in USM. Tools with smaller contact area yield better penetration rates allowing efficient flow of abrasive underneath. Choice of the tool material is also important as the tool has to withstand vibrations and excursion due to flow of the abrasive. Tough malleable materials such as alloy steels and stainless steels have been found to be suitable tool materials. The tool is made of low carbon or stainless steel to the shape of desired cavity.

1.3.2 Limitations of the Process

The major limitations of the process is its comparatively low metal cutting rates. The maximum metal removal rate is 3mm^3/sec and the power consumption is high. The depth of cylindrical holes is presently limited to 2.5 times the diameter of the tool. Wear of the tool increases the angle of the hole, while sharp corners become rounded. This implies that tool replacement is essential in the production of accurate blind holes. Also, the process is limited, in its present form to machine on surfaces of comparatively small size.

1.3.3 Recent Development

Recently a new development in Ultra-sonic Machining has taken place in which a tool impregnated with diamond dust is used and no slurry is used. The tool is oscillated at ultrasonic frequencies as well as rotated. If it is not possible to rotate the tool the workpiece may be rotated.

This innovation has removed some of the drawbacks of conventional process in drilling deep holes. For instance the hole dimensions can be kept within $\pm$ 0.125 mm. Holes upto 75mm depth have been drilled in ceramics wi hout any fall in the rate of machining as is experienced in the conventional process.

1.3.4 Applications

The simplicity of the process makes it economical for a wide range of applications such as:

1. Producing holes of round of such other shapes which can be provided to the cutting tool.
2. For making tungsten carbide and diamond wire drawing dies and dies for forging and extrusion processes.
3. In several machining operations like turning, threading, grinding, trapanning, and milling, etc.,
4. Machining of hard to machine and brittle materials.
5. In cutting threads in the components made of hard metals and alloys.
6. Enabling the dentist to drill a hole of any shape on the teeth without creating any pain.

1.3.5 Advantages of U.S.M.

1. Extremely hard and brittle materials can be easily machined.
2. Highly accurate profiles and good surface finish can be easily obtained.
3. The machined workpieces are free of stresses.
4. Metal removal cost is low.
5. Due to no heat generation in the process, the physical properties of the work material remain unchanged.

6. The operation is noiseless.
7. Operation of the equipment is quite safe.

1.3.6 Disadvantages of U.S.M.

1. Metal removal rate is low.
2. Initial equipment cost is higher than conventional machine tools.
3. Process does not suit for heavy metal removal.
4. The cost of tooling is also high.
5. Difficulties are faced in machining softer materials.
6. Power consumption is quite high.
7. For accurate machining, the tool needs to be replaced, due to high wear rate of tool.
8. For efficient cutting action, the slurry may have to be replaced periodically.
9. The size of cavity that can be machined is limited.

1.4 ABRASIVE JET MACHINING (A.J.M.) PROCESS

This process consists of directing a stream of fine abrasive grains, mixed with compressed air or gas at high pressure, through a nozzle on to the surface of the workpiece to be machined. These particles impinge on the work surface at high speed and the erosion caused by their impact enables the removal of metal. This process is mainly employed for such machining works which are difficult to machine, such as thin sections of hard metals and alloys, cutting of materials which are sensitive to heat damage, producing intricate holes, deburring, etching and polishing etc.

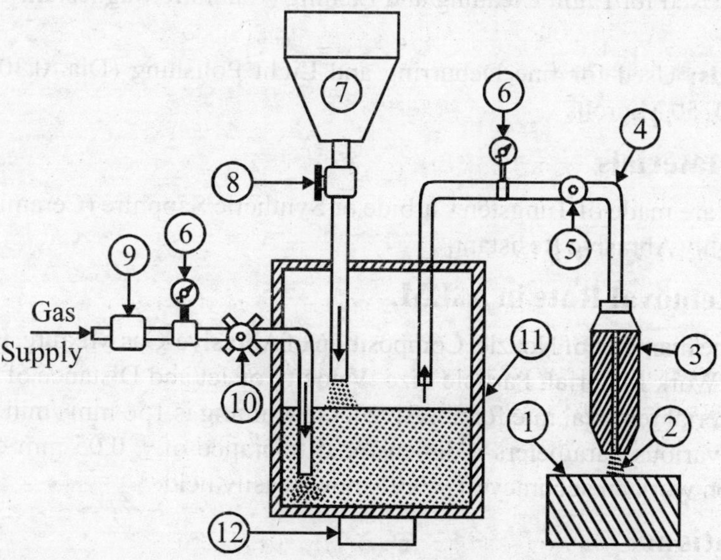

Fig. 1.2: Principle of a Abrasive Jet Machining 1. Workpiece, 2. Abrasive jet, 3. Nozzle, 4. Hose, 5. Control valve for jet flow, 6. Pressure gauge, 7. Hopper, 8. Regulator, 9. Filter, 10. Gas/Air regulator, 11. Mixing chamber, 12. Vibrating device.

Fine grained abrasive powder is filled in a vibrating chamber, called Mixing Chamber. The air or gas at high pressure (2 to 8.0 kg/cm^2) is forced into this chamber. A typical set-up for Abrasive Jet Machining (AJM) is shown in Fig.2.1. The abrasive particles are contained in a suitable holding device, like a Hopper, and fed into the Mixing Chamber.

A regulator is incorporated in this line to control the flow of abrasive particles. Compressed Air or High Pressure Gas (2-8 kg/cm^2) is supplied to the Mixing Chamber through a pipe line. This pipe line carries a Pressure Gauge and Regulator to control the gas flow and its pressure. The mixing chamber, carrying the abrasive particles, is vibrated (SOHz) and the Amplitude of these vibrations controls the flow of abrasive particles. These particles mix in the gas stream, travel further through a Hose and finally pass through the Nozzle Impacting the Work Surface at considerably high speed. This outgoing high speed stream of the mixture of Gas and Abrasive Particles is known as Abrasive Jet (V = 300m/min)

1.4.1 Variables in A.J.M. (Gases, Abrasives and Nozzle Materials) Gases

The carrier gas used in this process should be non-toxic, easily available, cheap and one that dries quickly. The gases commonly used are Air, Nitrogen, Carbondioxide.

Abrasives:

(*i*) **Aluminium Oxide:** Used for General Purpose Machining, Grooving and Cutting.

(*ii*) **Silicon Carbide (SIC):** Used for Faster Machining of Hard Materials

(*iii*) **Sodium-bi-Carbonate:** Used for fine finishing work

(*iv*) **Dolomite:** Used for Light Cleaning and Etching (Calcium Magnesium Carbonate)–200 Grit Size

(*v*) **Glass Beads:** Used for fine Deburring and Light Polishing (Dia. 0.30–0.60 mm) Size of Particles 10–50 Microns

1.4.2 Nozzle Materials

The nozzles used are made of Tungsten Carbide or Synthetic Sapphire (Ceramic) because these are required to be highly Abrasive Resistant.

1.4.3 Metal Removal Rate in A.J.M.

It depends upon the diameter of Nozzle, Composition of Abrasive-Gas Mixture, Hardness of Abrasive Particles and the Work Material, Particle Size, Velocity of Jet and Distance of Workpiece from the Jet. A typical material removal rate for abrasive jet machining is 156 mm^3/min in cutting glass with close control of various parameters a dimensional tolerance of $\pm$ 0.05 mm can be obtained. On normal production work an accuracy of $\pm$ 0.01 mm is easily held.

1.4.4 Applications

1. Machining of Brittle Materials (Glass, Ceramics, Refractories)
2. Cleaning and Cutting Operations on Germanium, Silicon, Quartz, Mica
3. Cutting Slots, Thin Sections, Contouring

4. Drilling and for Producing Shallow Cavities
5. Deburring and for Producing Intricate Shapes in Hard and Brittle Materials.
6. Cleaning and Polishing of Plastics and Nylon Components

1.4.5 Advantages

1. Low capital cost.
2. No direct contact between tool and work.
3. Heat generated not appreciable.
4. Brittle materials of thin sections can be easily machined.
5. Intricate cavities and holes of any shape may be machined in hard materials.
6. Good Accuracy can be obtained.

1.4.6 Disadvantages

1. Metal removal is slow.
2. Unsuitable for machining ductile materials.
3. Machining accuracy relatively poor.
4. Abrasive powder used in the process cannot be reused.
5. There is danger of abrasive particles getting embedded in the soft materials, hence cleaning is done after the operation.
6. Nozzle wear rate is high.

1.5 WATER JET MACHINING (W.J.M.) PROCESS

In this process, a high velocity water jet is made to impinge on to the workpiece. This jet pierces the work materials and performs a sort of slitting operation. Water under pressure, from a Hydraulic Accumulator is passed through the orifice of a Nozzle to increase its velocity. The nozzle orifice size (Dia) usually varies from 0.08 mm to 0.5 mm and the exit velocity of the water jet from the nozzle varies upto 920 m/sec. These high velocity jets can be used to cut relatively softer and non-metallic materials like paper boards, wood, plastics, asbestos, rubber and leather, etc.

A recent variation of this process, known as Hydrodynamics Jet Machining (H.J.M.) has been successfully used to machine almost all types of ferrous and non-ferrous metals and alloys. In this process, similar to A.J.M., abrasive particles are added to the high velocity Water Jet, which is made to impinge on the work material. The principle of Hydro-Dynamic Abrasive Jet Machining is shown in Fig. 1.3. In this process, the nozzle carries a Mixing Chamber (Abrasive Tube) at its end. The abrasive particles are thrown into the water jet coming out of the nozzle and the mixture of two (water and abrasives) comes out of the chamber (Tube) in the form of a High Velocity Water - Abrasive Jet to be directed on to the workpiece. The material is removed due to combined effect of the abrasion and impact. With the use of proper abrasive and adequate water pressure, any material can be cut through this process.

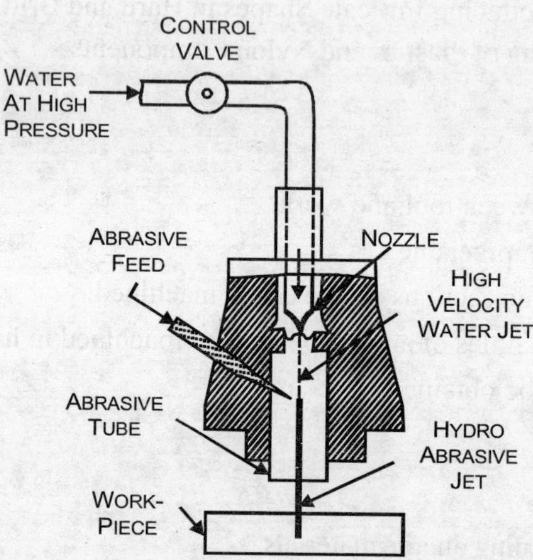

Fig. 1.3: Principle of Hydro-dynamic Jet Machining

It is reckoned that the cut (Slit) produced in the workpiece is lightly larger (0.025 mm) than the diameter of the jet. The water pressures used in the process vary from 2100 kg/cm^2 to 3500 kg/cm^2. Commonly used abrasives are Silica, Aluminium Oxide and Garnet and their grit sizes 60, 80, 100 and 120 are in general use. The mixing chamber (Abrasive tube) is usually made of extremely hard and wear resistant material like carbide. Usually a gap of 0.5 mm to 1.5 mm is necessary between the work surface and the tip of the tube.

REVIEW QUESTIONS

1. Explain the principle of Ultrasonic Machining with the help of neat diagram.
2. What are the main Advantages, Disadvantages and Applications of USM process?
3. Describe the mechanism of metal removal in USM and discuss the effects of following parameters on metal removal:

   (*i*) Amplitude, (*ii*) Frequency, (*iii*) Type of Abrasive, and (*iv*) Grain Size
4. What is Abrasive Jet Machining (AJM) process? Explain its principle of operation.
5. What are main Advantages, Disadvantages and Industrial Applications of AJM process?
6. What is Water Jet Machining (WJM) process? What are its main Applications?
7. Explain the principle of Hydrodynamic Jet Machining?
8. Describe at least three engineering applications of AJM.
9. What is the principle of Water Jet Machining?

1.6 ELECTROCHEMICAL MACHINING (E.C.M.) PROCESS

This process is a new field of metal removal which has bean developed on two well-known principles given by Faraday and Ohm. A shaped tool (Electrode) is used in the process, which forms Cathode. The workpiece forms Anode. A small gap (0.25mm) is maintained between the tool and workpiece and an electrolyte (Sodium nitrate solution) is pumped through it. Low Voltage Direct Current (3–50V) is employed which, in the presence of electrolyte, enables a controlled metal removal from the workpiece by Ion-Migration towards the tool. Deposition of ions on the tool is prevented by pumping the strong stream of electrolyte in the gap which flushes off the metallic ions from the cutting zone.

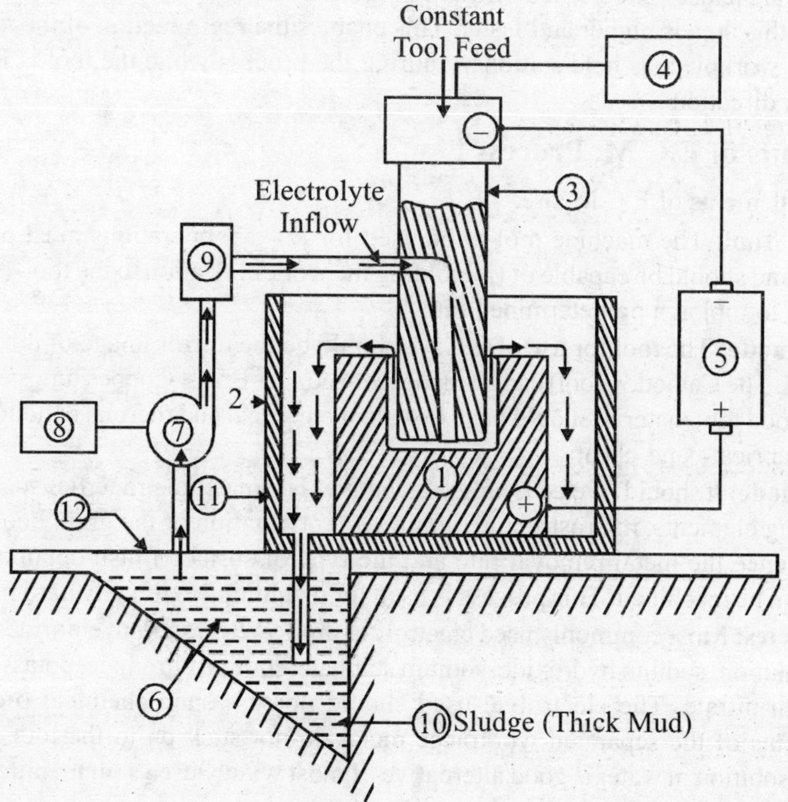

Fig. 1.4: Setup for ECM Process 1. Workpiece, 2. Tank, 3. Tool (Cathode), 4. Servomotor for controlled tool feed, 5. D.C. power supply, 6. Electrolyte, 7. Pump, 8. Motor for pump, 9. Filter for incoming electrolyte, 10. Sludge, 11. Down flow of used electrolyte, 12. Reservoir for electrolyte.

Fig. 1.4, shows a typical set-up of Electro-Chemical Machining. The electric current is of the order of 50 to 40,000 A at 3–50V D.C. for a current density of 20–300 A/cm^2, across a gap of 0.05–0.7mm between the tool and the workpiece. The electrolyte flows through this gap at a velocity of 30–40 m/sec forced by an inlet pressure of about 20 kgf/cm^2. The temperature of the electrolyte is maintained around 25–60°C. Suspended solids (Sludge) are removed from the electrolyte by setting, filtering and the filtered electrolyte is recirculated for use. Due to applied voltage the current flows through the electrolyte with +vely charged ions being attracted towards the Tool (Cathode) and –vely charged ones towards the workpiece (Anode). The electrochemical reaction, taking place due to this flow of ions, results in the removal of metal from the workpiece in the form of Sludge. This sludge is taken away from the gap by the flowing electrolyte alongwith it. The area where the tool and workpiece are closer experiences flow of higher current due to low resistance. The metal removal rate in this area is higher and faster. This enables the reproduction of the tool shape on the workpiece. The workpiece is held stationary during the process while the tool is fed at a constant speed in a linear direction.

1.6.1 Elements of E.C.M. Process

The important elements of E.C.M. are:

(i) **Machine Tool:** The machine tool to be used for E.C.M. operations must possess adequate stiffness and should be capable of (*i*) Holding the work in relation to the tool, (*ii*) Hold the tool, (*iii*) Feed to tool at a predetermined rate.

(ii) **Tool Cathode:** The tool for use of E.C.M. should be the mirror image of the workpiece to be machined. The Cathode (Tool) can be made from copper Brass, Copper-tungsten alloy, stainless steel. A good tool material should have excellent electrical and thermal conductivity, should be easy to fabricate and cheap.

(iii) **Work Anode:** It should be electrically conductive. The material properties such as the presence of alloying elements, microstructure, grain size, orientation of the grain boundaries, valency can influence the metal removal rate and the type of surface finish obtained Practically all metals can be machined. This process is used for machining extremely hard metals and alloys.

(iv) **Electrolytes:** Most commonly used electrolites are 15–20% sodium chloride in water, sodium nitrate solution, sodium hydroxide, sodium sulphate, sodium chromate, potassium chloride and potassium nitrate. The electrolyte used should possess such chemical properties that the constituents of the separated workpiece metal do not stick on to the tool surface. Sodium chloride solution in water is good alternative of most widely used sodium nitrate solution but is more corrosive.

(v) **Current and Voltage:** The electric current is of the order of 50 to 40,000 A at 3–50V D.C. for a current density of 20 to 300 A/cm^2 across a gap of 0.05-0.7 mm between the tool and the workpiece. Large current density in E.C.M. leads to rapid metal removal rack but it heats the electrolyte to a large extent. This results into large overcuts, poor surface finish and poor machining accuracy.

(vi) **Feed Rate:** E.C.M. is a self-adjusting process wherein for the given machining conditions, the tool work gap after some time approaches an equilibrium value. For E.C.M. with plane parallel electrodes and constant rate of feeding the equilibrium gap (G) is given by: $G_{Equilibrium}$ = (VSC)/*f*, where S is the specific metal removal rate *i.e.*, volume material removed per Amp. At large feeds the equilibrium gap would be small whereas, at low feeds the equilibrium gap is large. The concept of equilibrium gap in E.C.M. is very important and is widely used in Electrochemical Tooling Design.

(vii) Tool-work Gap: A small gap (0.05 to 0.7mm) is maintained between the tool and workpiece.

Metal Removal Rate: The Metal Removal Rate (MRR) is given by MRR = $\frac{EI}{F_P}$ m^3/sec. Where,

E = (Atomic weight N) Valency (*n*), I = Current in AMPs, F = Faraday Constant = 96.500 Columob = 26.8 Amp-hv., P = density, the feed rate of Electrode (*f*) is given by,

$f = \frac{V}{esh} \times \frac{E}{FP}$ m/sec where, V = Machining voltage – Volts, ρs = Specific resistance of electrolyte in ohm-m, h = total work gap in *m*. The Current Efficiency is given by

$$\eta = \frac{\text{Actual Metal Removed/Amp-Min}}{\text{Theoretical Metal Removal/Amp-min}} \times 100\%$$

Ex.1: Calculate the machining rate and the electrode feed rate when iron is electro-chemically machined using copper electrode and sodium chloride solution (specific resistance = 5.0 ohm-cm). The power supply data of the E.C.M. machine used are:

Supply Voltage = 18 V d.c., Current = 5000 A

A tool-work gap of 0.5 cm (constant) may be assumed. The current efficiency η can be taken as 100 per cent with the sodium chloride electrolyte.

For iron (anode), atomic weight, N = 56; valency, n = 2; Density, P = 7.87 g/cm^2

Sol.: According to formula, Metal Removal Rate,

$$MRR = \frac{EI}{FP} m^3/sec = \frac{56}{2} \times \frac{5000}{1} \times \frac{1}{96500} \times \frac{1}{7.87} \qquad \left(\because E = \frac{N}{n}\right)$$

$$= 3.67 \times 10^{-5} \times 5000 = 0.1835 cm^3/sec = 1.835 \times 10^{-7} m^3/sec$$

$$\text{Electrode Feed Rate, } f = \frac{V}{\rho s h} \times \frac{E}{F\rho} = \frac{18}{5 \times 0.05} \times \frac{3.67 \times 10^{-5}}{1} \text{ cm/sec.}$$

= 1.58 mm/min **Ans.**

Ex.2: In a certain electro-chemical dissolution process of iron, a metal removal rate of 3cm^3/min was desired. Determine the amount of current required for the process, assuming:

Atomic weight of iron, N = 56gm, Valency, $n = 2$

Density of iron, ρ = 7.8 gm/cm^3, F = 1,609 Amp-min

Sol.: We know that, MRR= EI/Fρ cm^3/sec.

$\therefore$ 3 = = (56 × *I*)/1,609 × 2 ×7.8 $\therefore$ *I* = (3 × 1609 × 7.8)/28 = 1344.6 Amp. **Ans.**

1.6.2 Chemistry of the Process

In the electrolytic circuit shown in Fig. 1.5, consider that iron is being machined electro-chemically using NaCl solution as electrolyte. When the current is switched on, the electrolyte (say $NaCl + H_2O$) gets ionised to the relationships, $NaCl \longrightarrow \overset{+}{Na} + \overset{-}{Cl}$; $H_2O \longrightarrow \overset{+}{H} + \overset{-}{OH}$. As Hydrogen ions reach the cathode they combine with the free electrons as follows resulting into evolution of Hydrogen gas $2H + 2e \longrightarrow H_2$ (Hydrogen evolution).

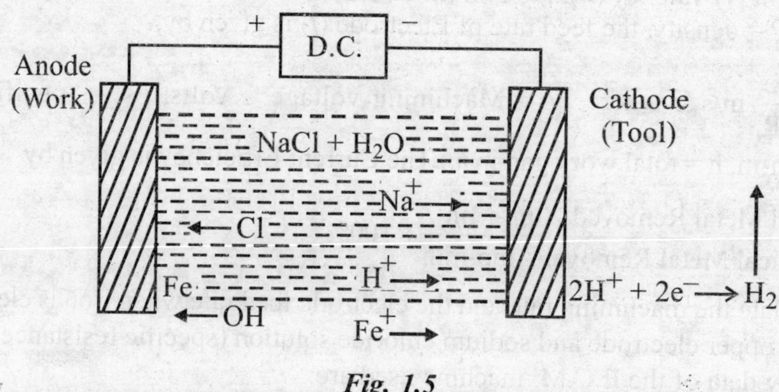

Fig. 1.5

Let us assume that we are machining pure iron by this method, the reactions that would occur are:

$$2\overset{+}{Na} + 2\overset{+}{O}H = 2NaOH; \quad \overset{++}{Fe} + 2\overset{-}{C}l = FeCl_2$$

$$2NaOH + FeCl_2 = 2NaCl + Fe(OH)_2$$

Thus in ECM of iron, using NaCl as the electrolyte, iron is removed as $Fe(OH)_2$ and the sodium chloride is reovered back. The iron hydroxide produced during the process must be removed continusouly from the electrolyte by filtration before it is recirculated.

1.6.3 Accuracy of E.C.M.

There are a number of factors which govern the accuracy of the parts produced by E.C.M. The major ones are: (*i*) Machining Voltage, (*ii*) Feed rate of Electrode (Tool), (*iii*) Temperature of Electrode, (*iv*) Concentration of Electrolyte.

Under ideal conditions with properly designed tooling ECM is capable of holding tolerances of the order of ± 0.02 mm and less. On a good machine, tolerance can be maintained on a production basis in the region of ± 0.02 to 0.04 mm. As a general rule, the more complex the shape of the work, the more difficult is to hold tight tolerances. E.C.M. results in internal radii greater than 0.2 mm and external radii of the order of 0.05 mm.

1.6.4 Surface Finish

Surface finish in E.C.M. is of the order of 0.2 to 0.8 micron (CLA), depending on the work material and the electrolyte used, and no burns or sharp edges are left on the workpiece. Taper is of the order of 0.010 mm for 10 mm depth and the side over-cut is about 0.1 to 0.2 mm.

1.6.5 Applications

1. Machining of Hard to Machine and Heat Resisting Alloys.
2. Machining of Blind Holes and Pockets (Forging Dies).
3. Machining of Complicated Profiles (Jet Enging Blades, Turbine Blades, Turbine Wheels).
4. Drilling Small Deep Holes (Nozzles).
5. Machining of cavities and holes of irregular shapes.
6. Deburring of parts.
7. Machining of Turgsten Carbide.
8. Almost all conducting materials can be machined by this method.
9. Multiple hole drilling, Trepanning, Broaching, Grinding and Polishing operations.

1.6.6 Advantages

1. Intricate and complex shapes can be machined easily.
2. Any good electrically conducting material can be machined.
3. Machining ability is independent of the mechanical properties of the work material.
4. Metal removal rate is quite high for High Strength-Temperature-Resistant (HSTR) materials in comparison to traditional machining.
5. Tool wear is nearly absent.
6. Extremely thin metal sheets can be easily machined without any danger of damage or distortion.
7. The machined work surface is free from Stresses.
8. No cutting forcus are involved in the process.
9. High surface finish (0.2 to 0.8 microns) can be obtained.
10. It is an accurate process and close tolerances of the order of 0.05 mm can be easily obtained.

1.6.7 Economics (Disadvantages)

1. Power consumption is High.
2. Materials which are non-conductors of electrecity cannot be machined.
3. Corrosion and rusting of workpiece, machine tool, and fixtures etc., by electrotyte is a constant menance.
4. Required initial investment is quite high.
5. Extremely fine corner radii, say less than 0.2 mm, cannot be produced.
6. Designing and fabrication of Tools is relatively more difficult.
7. Longer floor space is required.

8. Specially designed Fixtures are required to hold the workpiece in position, because it may be displaced due to pressure of the flowing electrolyte.
9. A constant monitoring is required to suitably vary the tool feed Rate and supply pressure of electrolyte so as to avoid formation of cavitation.

1.7 ELECTROCHEMICAL GRINDING (E.C.G.) PROCESS

It is also known as Electrolytic Grinding or Anode Grinding. In this process, machining is affected both by the Grinding Action and by the Electronchemical Process. Hence it may be called Mechanically Assisted Electrochemical Machining. The specific use of this process is in grinding such materials which cannot be easily shaped due to their extreme Hardness or Too High Tensile Strength, such as cemented carbide, hardened steels and some steel alloys. The process consists of connecting the grinding wheel to negative terminal and the workpiece to the positive terminal to make the farmer a Cathode and the latter Anode. The power supply unit is of D.C. and provides an automatic voltage adjustment between 5–20V (50–200A). The coolant used in the process is an Electro-conductive Electrolyte. The Electrolyte, which is usually sodium nitrate, sodium nitrite, sodium chloride, and potassium nitrite, with a concentration of 0.150 to 0.30 kg/litre of water, is passed through the nozzle in the machining zone in order to complete the electrical bridge between the anode and the cathode. Grinding wheel runs at a surface speed of about 1500m/min.

On the periphery of the grinding wheel are attached the the abrasive particles which act as insulators, preventing the direct contact between the wheel and workpiece. A constant gap of 0.025 mm is maintained into which a stream of electrolyte is directed. The electric current between the wheel and workpiece flows through the electrolyte and the metal removal from the workpiece is through electrolytic action. The abrasive particles on the surface of the wheel remove the decomposed material to provide a fine surface finish and adequate dimensional control. With the rotation of grinding wheel, the metal is removed from the workpiece by the simultaneous electrolytic (90%) and abrasive (10%) action.

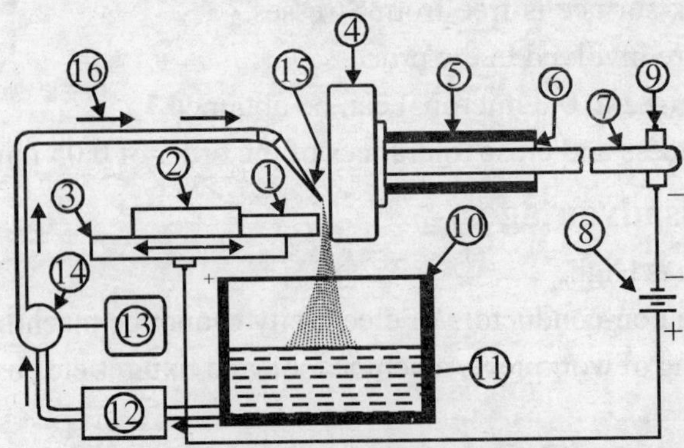

Fig. 1.6: Set-up for ECG Process 1. Workpiece, 2. Fixture, 3. Work table, 4. Grinding wheel, 5. Insulation, 6. Sleeve, 7. Spindle, 8. D.C. power source, 9. Contact bushes, 10. Tank for electrolyte, 11. Electrolyte, 12. Filter, 13. Motor for pump, 14. Pump, 15. Nozzle, 16. Direction of electrolyte flow.

A typical set-up of E.C.G. is shown in Fig. 1.6. The grinding wheel mounted on a spindle, rotates on suitable bearings. The workpiece is held on the machine table in a Suitable Fixture. The table can be moved forward and backward to feed the work or to withdraw it. The grinding wheel and spindle are insulated from the rest of the machine by using an insulating Sleeve. Electrolyte from the tank is pumped into the gap between the wheel and the workpiece. Current flows from the Cathode (Grinding Wheel) to the Anode (Workpiece) through the Electrolyte. This leads to an Electrochemical Oxidation on the work surface. This oxide film so formed is removed by the Grinding. Wheel producing a highly accurate and finished surface. The short circuiting between the wheel and work is prevented due to point contact made by fine abrasive particles.

The grinding wheels used are of conventional shape and structure. Metal bond, diamond grit wheels are used for grinding Tungsten Carbide Tips. Carbon bond wheels are used upon the hard alloy steels such as Stainless Steels. Wheel wear is negligible because the greatest part of the cutting action is electrolyte (90%) and little dressing is necessary. The Grinding Machine is similar in design to Surface Grinder and Tool and Cutter Grinder.

1.7.1 Surface Finish

The surface finish is held in the range of 0.2 to 0.4 micron on carbide and 0.4 to 0.8 micron on steel. Sharp corners are difficult to obtain and a minimum radius of 0.2 mm cannot be avoided unless a final pass without electrolytic action is used.

1.7.2 Accuracy

Because there is a very little abrasive action this process does not leave fine scratches which may impair the finish and leave stress raisers. Tolerances of about ± 0.02 are held on rather complex grinding operations. For closer tolerances, the proportion of material removed by abrasive should be increased.

1.7.3 Applications of E.C.G.

Any material which is electrically conductive may be ground by the electrolytic process, but its most useful application is concerned with hardened steel, cemented carbides and similar materials. This is mainly applied to resharpening and reconditioning of carbide tools and other materials that are difficult to grind. As the grinding pressure is low, it is possible to grind and cut thin sections such as stainless steel, cobalt titanium, cements and thin wall tubing of difficult materials (injection syringe) without distortion or burr.

1.7.4 Advantages of E.C.G.

1. Negligible wear on the grinding wheel (Tool).
2. Work is free of surface cracks and distortion as heat is not generated in the process.
3. Increased wheel life.
4. For hard materials like cobalt, tungsten etc., the rate of metal removal is much higher than conventional grinding.
5. As compared to conventional grinding, very little cutting force is applied to the workpiece.
6. Work material is not subjected to any structural change.

7. Fairly high dimensional accuracy, of the order of 0.01 mm can be achieved.
8. Considerable saving in wheel dressing time.
9. Fairly good surface finish is obtained.

1.7.5 Disadvantages

1. High initial cost.
2. High power consumption.
3. Only electrically conductive materials can be machined.
4. Preventive measures are always required against corrosion by the electrolyte.
5. In general grinding work, metal removal rate is lower than conventional grinding.

1.8 CHEMICAL MACHINING (CHM) PROCESS

In this process, the metal is removed from the workpiece through a Controlled Chemical Attack with Acids or Alkalies (Etchant Solution) for producing desired shapes and dimensions from the selected portions or from the entire surface. The metal is gradually transformed into metallic salt by chemical reaction and is ultimately removed in this form. Areas from where material is not to be removed are protected by an Echant resistant material, known as 'Maskant' or 'Resist'. Nearly all the material, from metals to ceramics, can be chemically machined.

The component to be machined is first cleaned in a solution of mild alkaline solution at 80 to 90°C, followed by washing in clean water, one of the roughest method is to coat the component all over by spraying or dipping. This removes dust and oil. The cleaning ensures a good adhesion of the coating or masking agent which is applied to protect the portions which are not to be machined. After cleaning the component is dried and coated with the maskant material which may be cut and peel, photoresist or screen-print, type. Finally, the metal is removed by etching. The process can be suitably applied to different types of operations. Such as milling, blanking and engraving. The different chemical machining processes can thus be classified as:

1. Chemical Milling, 2. Chemical Blanking, and 3. Chemical engraving.

Chemical Machining Processes are mainly used when either it is impracticable or extremely difficult to employ the coventional machining methods due to very thin sections or complex shapes of the parts to be machined or extreme hardness, brittleness or toughness of the workpiece material. The resists used are of three types:

1. **Cut and Peel Type:** These are used when very critical dimensional tolerances are not required. They are applied by dip or spray method.
2. **Photographic Resists:** These are used for thin sections are components requiring closer dimensional tolerances. They can be applied by dip, roll coating or spray method.
3. **Screen Resists:** These are generally used for relatively shorter parts having flat surfaces or otherwise simple contours.

1.9 CHEMICAL MILLING

Chemical milling is the controlled dissolution of work material by contact with a strong chemical reagent. This process was originally developed by American Aircraft Industries for preparing the parts having large curved surfaces and thin sections. Many difficulties were felt in preparing such a surface by conventional milling operation. The process is carried out in the sequence of (*i*) Cleaning, (*ii*) Masking, (*iii*) Etching, and (*iv*) Demasking.

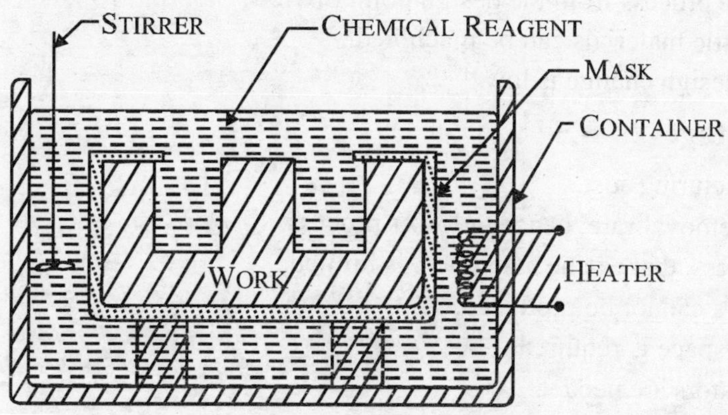

Fig. 1.7

The thoroughly cleaned workpiece is covered with a shippable, chemically resistant mask. Areas where chemical action is desired are outlined on the workpiece is next submerged in the chemical reagent to remove material simultaneously from all exposed surfaces. The solution should be stirred or the workpiece should agitated for more uniform etching. Increasing the temperature would also expedite the process. The machine workpiece is next washed are rinsed and the remaining mask is removed. The schematic diagram of a typical set up is shown in Fig. 1.7.

2. **Chemical Blanking :** In this process, the metal is totally removed from certain areas by chemical action. The process is used chiefly on their sheets and foils. Almost any metal can be worked by this process, however, it is not recommended for materials thinner than 2 mm.

The workpiece is cleaned, degreased and pickled by acid or alkalis. The cleaned metal is dried and photoresist material is applied to the workpiece by dipping, whirl coating or spraying. It is then dried and curved. The technique of photography has been used to produce etchant resistant images, in photo resist materials. This surface is now exposed to the light through the negative. After exposure, the image is developed. The treated metal is next put into a machine. The etching solution may be hydrofluoric acid. After 1 to 15 min, the unwanted metal has been eaten away, and the finished part is ready for immediate ringins to remove the etchant. Printed circuit cards, other engraving operations and blanking of intricate designs can be suitably made by chemical blanking by using photoresist maskants.

1.9.1 Advantages

1. Tooling cost is very low.
2. Both faces of the workpiece can be machined simultaneously.
3. Tooling time is substantially reduced.

4. The material is not subjected to usual defects (Hardening, cracks).
5. The part produced is free of burrs.
6. Complex contours can be easily machined.
7. It is a flexible process from the design point of view.
8. Hard and brittle materials can be machined.
9. The cost of design change is low.

1.9.2 Disadvantages

1. High manufacturing cost.
2. Low metal removal rate, hence, a lower process.
3. Metal thickness, that can be machined, is limited.
4. Sharp corners cannot be produced.
5. Larger floor space is required.
6. Skilled operators are needed.

1.9.3 Applications

1. Nearly all metals can be chemically machined, however the depth of cut has a practical limit of 6.5 to 12.5 mm.
2. Large shallow areas are specially suitable for chemical milling.
3. Thin sheets, formed sheets and delicate cuts are patricularly suited to this process.
4. One of the major applications of chemical machining is in the manufacture of burr free, intricate stampings.
5. The surface finish obtained in the process is in the range of 0.5 to 2 microns.

REVIEW QUESTIONS

1. Explain the principle of Electrochemical Machining (ECM) process with the help of neat diagram.
2. What are main Advantages, Disadvantages and Appilcations of ECM?
3. How does the metal removal take place in the Electrolytic Grinding both, by Abrasion and Chemical Deposition?
4. How the Metal Removal and Feed Rates for Alloys can be calculated in ECM?
5. Discuss the main requirements of Electrolyte and Tool Material for use in ECM.
6. With neat diagram, explain the process of Electrochemical Grinding (ECG)
7. What are the specific advantages of using chemical machining over electrochemical machining? Give some practical applications of the chemical machining process.
8. (*i*) What are the factors on which the selection of a resist for use in chemical machining depend?

   (*ii*) Distinguish between cut and peel resists and photographic resists.
9. Write short notes on:

(*i*) The economics of electrochemical machining

(*ii*) The effect of high temperature and pressure of electrolyte in the ECM process.

(*iii*) Applications of Electrochemical Grinding Process.

1.10 THERMAL METAL REMOVAL PROCESSES

Several machining processes involving the application of very intense local heat have come into use in recent years. In these processes, the material is removed by melting or vapourizing small areas at the surface of workpiece. The processes in which metal removal is based on thermal principles are:

1. Electric Discharge Machining (EDM).
2. Plasma Arc Machining (PAM).
3. Electron Beam Machining (EBM).
4. Laser Beam Machining (LBM).
5. Hot Machining.

1.11 ELECTRIC DISCHARGE MACHINING (E.D.M.) PROCESS

It is also known as Spark Erosion Machining or Spark Machining. In this process, the metal removal takes place due to Erosion caused by the Electric Spark. This process may be used for machining any material which is an electrical conductor. The rate of metal removal and the resulting surface finish can be controlled by proper variation in the energy and the duration of spark discharge. A liquid dielectric, like kerosene oil, Transformer oil, Paraffin oil, Lubricating oil, is always used in the process.

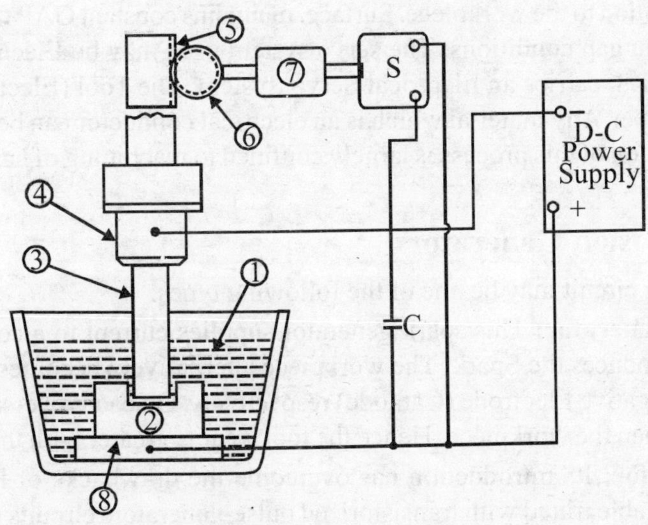

Fig. 1.8: General Setup for an EDM Process. 1. Dielectric, 2. Workpiece, 3. Tool, 4. Tool head, 5. Rack, 6. Pinion, , 7. Reduction gear box, 8. Base. C-Capacitor, S-Servo control

The general setup for an E.D.M. process is shown in Fig. 1.8. The main elements of this setup include a Power Supply Source, a Dielectric Medium, Workpiece, a Tool, Servocontrol, Speed Reduction Gear Box, a Rack and Pinion mechanism for Tool Feed, an Electric Circuit to generate discharge. The workpiece is connected to the positive (Anode) terminal and the tool to the negative (Cathode) terminal of the D.C. Electric Supply Source.

The principle involved in the process is that the workpiece and the electrode (Tool) are separated by a gap (0.05 mm - 0.05 mm) called Spark Gap. This gap is filled by the Electrolyte, which breaks down when a proper voltage is applied between these two. When a circuit voltage of 50V to 450V is applied, the dielectric breaks down and electrons start flowing from the Cathode, due to electrostatic field, and the gap is Ionised. The consequent drop in resistance and discharge of electric energy results in an electrical breakdown. The Electric Spark so caused directly impinges on the surface of the workpiece. It takes only a few micro seconds to complete the cycle and the spark discharges hit the Anode (Workpiece) with considerable force and velocity, resulting in the development of a very high temperature (around 10,000°C) on the spot hit by the discharges. This forces the metal to melt, and a portion of it may be vapourised even. These vapourised or melted particles of the metal are thrown into the gap by the electrostatic and electromagetic forces, from where they are driven away by the following liquid dielectric.

The erosion takes place on both, the tool as well as workpiece, but the former is eroded much less as compared to the latter. It is because the tool tip is subjected to compressive forces due to the electric and magnetic fields, resulting in a slower erosion of the metal from its surface. The rate of metal removal depends upon the discharge current, duration of pulse and rate of pulse repetition. The machining speed is usually mentioned in terms of the amount of metal removal in cm^3/min.

In E.D.M. system, the Gap Control is affected through the Servo System. This system correctly locates the tool in relation to the workpiece. Surface, maintains constant GAP throughout the operation and senses changes in gap conditions. The servo system used may be Electrical or Hydraulic. The setup shown in Fig. 1.8, carries an Electrical Servo System. The Tool (Electrode) used is generally made of Brass or copper. Any material which is an electrical conductor can be machined through this process. The application of this process is largely confined to machining of hard materials only due to economic reasons.

1.11.1 Spark Erosion Generators

The spark generating circuit may be one of the following types:

(*a*) **Relaxation Generator:** This spark generator supplies current to a condenser, the discharge from which produces the Spark. The workpiece alternatively becomes the Positive Electrode (Anode) or Negative Electrode (Cathode) respectively. On each reversal of Polarity the tool is eroded more than the workpiece. Hence the tool wear is greater with this type of arrangement.

(*b*) **Pulse Generator:** Its introduction has overcome the drawbacks of Relaxation Generators. These are available, fitted with transistorized pulse-generators circuits in which reverse pulses are eliminated. These generators consist of electronic switching units which let the current pass periodically. These generators possess the means of accurate control over discharge duration, pause time and the current. These factors determine the overcut and hence the accuracy and surface finish.

1.11.2 Dielectric Fluids

The essential requirement of a dielectric fluid to be used in E.D.M. process are that:

1. They should have high dielectric strength.
2. They should breakdown electrically in the shortest possible time once the breakdown voltage has been reached.
3. Rapidly quench the spark or deionize the spark gap after the discharges have accured.
4. Provide an effective cooling medium.
5. Be capable of carrying away the swarf particles, in suspension, away from the working gap.
6. Have a good degree of fluidity.
7. Be cheap and easily available.

Light hydrocarbon oils seem to satisfy these requirements best of all. The common dielectrics used are Kerosene oil, Paraffin oil, Transformer oil or their mixture and certain aqueous solutions. Water, beining an electrical conductor, gives a metal removal rate of only about 40% of that obtained when using paraffin as a dielectric.

The dielectric should be filtered before reuse so that chip contamination of the fluid will not affect machining accuracy.

1.11.3 Electrodes for Spark Erosion

The Electrode (Tool) used is generally made of Brass or Copper, although some other materials like cast Iron, Tungsten, Graphite, Steel, alloys of silver and tungsten, etc., have also been used in some machining operations. The tool material selected should be easy to machine, have a high wear resistance, ensure faster metal removal, should be a good electrical conductor and tooling costs should reduce due to its use. The tool is made slightly undersize for inside machining and oversize for outside machining.

The shape of the tool will be basically the same as that of the product desired except that an allowance is made for the side clearance and overcut. For Broaching small holes, solid rods may be used but for larger ones, hollow tools are preferred. Dielectric may then be pumped through hollow tool. If an object is having a geometrical shape or is having symmetry about some axis, a tool equal to only a part of the object will be sufficient for complete machining of the object. Such segmented tools are specially useful for machining complex shapes that do not require close accuracy. It may be convenient to use a series of simpler tool rater than a complex single tool, to produce a particular cavity.

The tool wear is a function of the rate of metal removal, material of workpiece, current setting, machining area, gap between the tool and the workpiece and the polarity of the tool. It has been found that the higher the tool material melting point, the less the tool wear.

1.11.4 Machining Accuracy

Tolerance value of ±0.05 mm could be easily achieved by E.D.M. in normal production. By close control of the several variables a tolerance of ±0.03 mm could be achieved. A typical taper value is about 0.005 to 0.05 mm per 100mm depth. The taper effect decreases substantially to zero after about 75 mm penetration. An overcut of 5 to 100 micron is produced, depending upon finishing or roughing. The best surface finish that can be economically achieved on steel is 0.4 micron. In 'no wear' machining, using graphite electrode a surface finish withing 3.2 miron can be achieved.

1.11.5 Applications of E.D.M.

The E.D.M. process is used for the manufacture of tools having complicated profiles due to the ease with which hard metals and alloys can be machined. Other applications include resharpening of cutting tools and broaches, trepanning of holes with straight or curved axes, machining of cavities for dies. The E.D.M. provides economic advantages for making stamping tools, wire drawing and extrusion dies, header dies, forging dies and intricate mould cavities. It has been extremely used for machining of exotic materials used in aerospace industries, refrcatory metals, hard carbides, and hardenable steels. Delicate workpiece like copper parts for fitting into the vacuum tubes can be produced by this method.

1.11.6 Over cut

Overcut is the distance the spark will penetrate the workpiece from the tool and remove metal from the workpiece. Theoretically, it is slightly larger than the gap between the end of the tool and the workpiece. This overcut is generally 0.025 to 0.2 mm, on all surfaces. Overcut causes internal corners on the workpiece to have fillets with radii equal to the overcut. The radius of the cavity produced in the workpiece will be slightly larger than the radius of the tool nose.

In an E.D.M. machine, sparks are usually produced by successive switching on and off of the direct current and the spark thus produced wonders over the work surface.

1.11.7 Flushing

Flushing is the correct circulation of dielectric fluid between the electrode and the wrokpiece. The machining efficiency is highly dependent on the correct layout and adjustment of the flushing system. If eroded particles are not flushed thoroughly, they act as obstacles in the gap, reducing the dielectric strength, so that discharges of low energy can develop. Consequently, the material removal rate is affected. Based on the problem to be solved, pressure flushing, suction flushing and side flushing method may be used.

1.12 LASER BEAM MACHINING (L.B.M.) PROCESS

Laser stands for "Light Amplification by Stimulated Emission of Radiation". Focussing of the stimulated light on the workpiece results into very high surface temperature. The metal removal takes place due to melting and evaporation. The energy density of the laser beam is very high (4.6×10^9 w/cm^2) and with this high energy density it is possible to melt and vapourise any material. Normally Laser is used for microdrilling, and micro-welding because of low efficiency and high energy inputs.

The setup consists of a stimulating light source (Like Xenon Flash Lamp) and a Laser Rod. The light radiated from the Flash Lamp is focused on to the Laser Rod (Laser Tube), from where it is reflected and accelerated in the path. This light is emitted in the form of a slightly divergent Beam. A Lens is incorporated suitably in the path of this Beam of Light which converges and focuses the light beam on to the workpiece to be machined. This concentration of Laser Beam on the workpiece melts the work material and vaporises it. It is a very costly method and can be employed only when it is not feasible to machine a workpiece through other methods.

Fig. 1.9 shows the setup for Laser Beam Machining. It mainly consists of a Laser Tube, a pair of Mirrors—one at each end of the tube, a Flash Tube or Lamp (Energy Source), an Amplifying Source (Laser), a Power Supply Source, a Cooling System and a Lens (Focussing Source). The mainset up is fitted in an Enclosure, which carries a highly reflective surface inside.

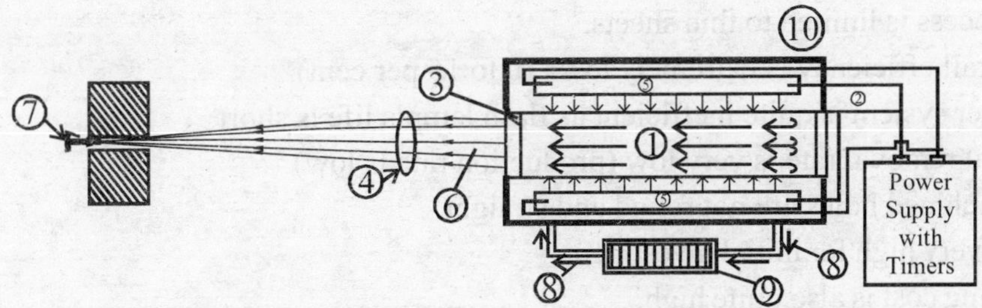

Fig. 1.9: A Laser Beam Setup 1. Ruby laser tube, 2. Total reflecting mirror, 3. Partial reflecting mirror, 4. Lens, 5. Flash tube (Xenon flash lamp), 6. Monochromatic light output, 7. Vaporised particles of work material, 8. Coolant flow, 9. Cooling system, 10. Enclosure

In operation, the optical energy (Light) is thrown by the Flash Lamp on to the Laser Tube (Ruby Rod). This excites the atoms of the inside media, which absorb the radiation of incoming light energy. This results in the to and fro travel of light between the two reflecting mirrors. But, the Partial Reflecting Mirror does not reflect the total light back and a part of it goes out in the form of a coherent stream of Monochromatic light. This hightly amplified stream of light is focussed through a Lens, which Coverges it to a chosen point on the workpiece. This high intensity converged Laser Beam, when falls on the workpiece, melts the workpiece, material, vaporises it almost instantaneously and penetrates into it. Thus it can be called a type of thermal cutting process.

The Lasing Medium or Laser used in the process can be of Solid or Gaseous type. The solid type are special glass rods carrying reflective coatings at their end faces. They can provide short duration laser beam only. Against these, the Gaseous Type, produce continuous Laser Beams and are, therefore, very suitable for welding and cutting operations.

1.12.1 Advantages of L.B.M.

1. Any material can be easily machined.
2. No involvement of cutting forces.
3. No tool wear.
4. Process can be effectively used for Welding of Dissimilar Metals as well.

5. Small heat effected zone around the machined surface.
6. Very small holes and cuts can be made with fairly high degree of accuracy.

1.12.2 Accuracy

The Laser is best used for cutting as well as for Drilling. Accuracy in profile cutting with numerical control or photoelectric tracer is about ±0.1 mm. The machined surface is normally rough and has a recast texture.

1.12.3 Limitations

One of the main limitations of the laser that it cannot be used to cut metals that have high heat conductivity or high reflectively, *e.g.*, Al, Cu and their alloys. In addition, the process has the following disadvantages:

1. The process is limited to thin sheets.
2. Its overall efficiency is extremely low (10 to 15 per cent).
3. The laser system is quite inefficient as flash lamp's life is short.
4. Material removal rate is very low (production rate is low)
5. The machined holes are not round and straight.
6. Cost is very high for initial investment.
7. Operating cost is also quite high.
8. Highly skilled operations are needed.
9. Cannot be effectively used to machine highly heat conductive and reflective materials.

1.13 PLASMA ARC MACHINING (PAM) PROCESS

When a flowing gas is heated to a sufficiently high temperature (above 5500°C) to become partially Ionized, it is known as 'Plasma'. This is virtually a mixture of Free Electrons, Positively Charged Ions and Neutral Atoms. The temperature of the central part of Plasma goes as high as between 11000°C to 30,000°C, where the gas is completely ionised. Plasma Arc Machining is a material removal process in which the material is removed by directing a high velocity jet of high temperature (11,000 to 30,000°C) ionised gas on the workpiece surface by means of a well designed Plasma Arc Cutting Torch (Fig. 1.10). This Jet melts the metal of the workpiece and displaces the molten metal away from its path. The heating of workpiece material is not due to any chemical reaction but on account of the continuous attack of electrons which transfer the heat energy of high temperature ionised gas to the work material. This process can be safely used for machining any metal, including those which can be subjected to chemical reaction.

As shown in Fig. 1.10, the Plasma Arc Cutting Torch carries a Tungsten Electrode fitted in a small chamber. This electrode is connected to the –ve terminal of D.C. power supply source and, therefore, acts as a cathode. The other (+ve) terminal of the power supply is connected to the Nozzle formed near the bottom of the chamber. The Nozzle acts as an Anode. On one side of the torch is provided a passage for the supply of gas into the chamber. In the Plasma Torch, a volume of gas such as H_2, N_2, O_2 etc., is passed through the small passage where a high frequency spark (Arc) is maintained between the tungsten Electrode (Cathode) and the Copper Nozzle (Anode), both are water cooled. The high velocity Electrons, generated by arc, collide with gas molecules and produce dissociation of diatomic molecules of the gas resulting in Ionization of the atoms and causing large amounts of the thermal energy to be liberated. The Plasma forming gas is forced through a Nozzle Duct of the torch in such a manner as to stabilise the Arc. Much of the heating of the gas takes place in the constructed region of the nozzle duct resulting into relatively high exit gas velocity and very high core temperature upto 16000°C. The relatively Plasma Jet melts the workpiece material and the High Velocity Gas Stream effectively blows the molten metal away.

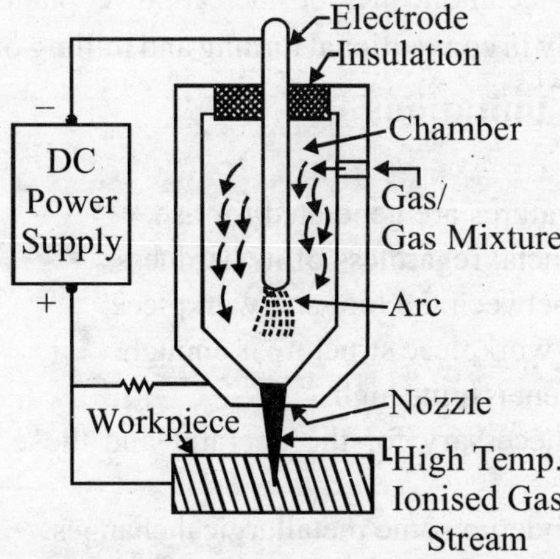

Fig. 1.10: Principle of Plasma Arc Machining.

The depth of heat affected zone depends on the work material, its thickness and cutting speed. On a workpiece of 25mm thickness the heat affected zone is about 4mm and it is less at high cutting speeds. Typical flow rate of the gas is 2 to 11 m^3/hr. Direct Current, rated at about 400V and 200 kW output is normally required. Arc current ranges between 150 and 1000A for a cutting rate of 250 to 1700 mm/min.

The choice of a particular gas for use in this process depends on the expected quality of finish on the cut surface and economic considerations. Any gas or gas-mixture which does not adversely affect the electrode or the workpiece materials can be safely used. Rate of flow of the gas will vary directly as the thickness of the workpiece.

There is also a provision of water circulation around the torch so that the electrode and the nozzle both remain water cooled. A strong Arc is struck between Electrode (Cathode) and the Nozzle (Anode) and the gas is forced into the chamber. As the gas molecules collide with the high velocity electrons of the arc, the former gets Ionised and a very large amount of heat energy is evolved. The flow of gas is so controlled that the arch remains stable. The high velocity stream of Hot Ionised Gas, called Plasma, is directed on to the workpiece to melt its material and also blow it away.

1.13.1 Accuracy

This is a roughing operation to an accuracy of about 1.5 mm with corresponding surface finish. Accuracy on the width of slots and diameter of holes is ordinarily from ±0.8mm on 6 to 30 mm thick plates and +30mm on 100 to 150 mm thick plates.

1.13.2 Applications of PAM

This is chiefly used to cut stainless steel and Aluminium alloys, particularly their profile cutting. With feasibility of its use under water, it is used in shipyards.

Other industries using this technique include nuclear power plants, chemical industries, etc.

It has been used sucessfully in conventional turning and milling of 'hard to machine' materials.

1.13.3 Advantages and Limitations

1. A faster process.
2. Excessively high temperatures are generated for use.
3. Can be used to cut any metal regardless of its hardness.
4. There being no contact between the tool and workpiece.
5. Only a simply supported workpiece structure is enough.
6. Initial cost of the equipment is quite high.
7. Safety precautions are necessary for the operator and those in near-by areas. This adds additional cost.
8. The work surface may undergo some metallurgical changes.

1.14 ELECTRON BEAM MACHINING (E.B.M.) PROCESS

1.14.1 Generation and Control of Electron Beam

It is a process of machining materials with the use of a high velocity beam of Electrons. The workpiece is held in a vacuum chamber and the Electron Beam focussed on to it magnetically. As the Electrons strike the workpiece, their Kinetic Energy is converted into Heat. This concentrated heat raises the temperature of workpiece material and vaporises a small amount of it, resulting in removal of metal from the workpiece. The reason for using a vacuum chamber is that, if otherwise, the beam electrons will collide with gas molecules and will scatter.

The main elements of Electron Beam Machining set up are shown in Fig. 1.11. The complete E.B.M. setup is enclosed in a vacuum chamber (10^{-5} mm of Hg-vacuum). This chamber carries a door, through which the workpiece is placd over the Table. The door is then closed and sealed. The Electron Gun, which is mainly responsible for emission of electrons, consists of three main parts; a Tungsten Filament, the Grid Cup and the Anode. The Filament is connected to the –ve terminal of the D.C. Power Supply to act as Cathode, and the Anode to the +ve terminal. The filament wire is heated to a temperature of about 2500°C in the vacuum. With the result, a cloud of electrons is emitted by the filament, which is directed by the Grid Cup to travel downwards. As the electrons are attracted by the anode, they pass through its aperture in the form of a controlled beam without colliding with it.

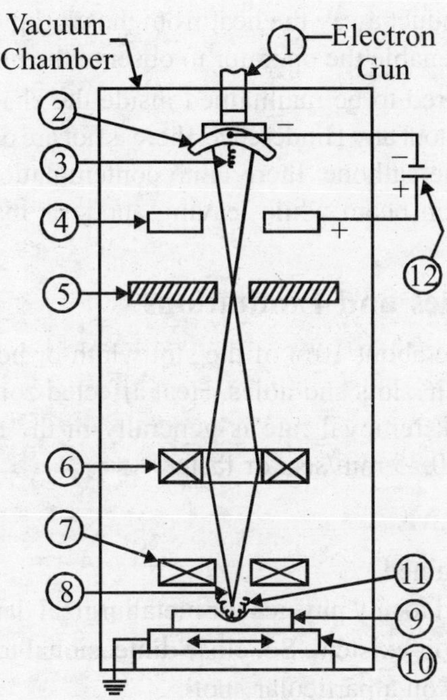

Fig. 1.11: Setup for Electron Beam Machining 1. Electrons gun, 2. Grid cup, 3. Tungsten filament (Cathode), 4. Anode, 5. Diaphragm, 6. Focussing lens (electromagnetic), 7. Deflector coil, 8. Electron stream (Beam), 9. Workpiece, 10. Table, 11. Work area being beated, melted and vaporised, 12. D.C. Power supply

1.14.2 Theory of Electron Beam Machining

A potential difference of 50 to 150 KV is maintained between the Filament and the Anode. As such, the electrons passing through the Anode are accelerated to achieve as high velocity as around two-third of light. The maximum velocity attained by the Electrons, while passing out of Anode, is maintained by them till such time as they strike the workpiece. It becomes possible because the electrons travel through the vacuum.

This high Velocity Electron Stream, after leaving the Anode, passes through the Tungsten Diaphragm and them through the Focussing Lens (Electromagnetic). By then, the stream is quite aligned and the Focussing Lens manages to focuss it precisely on to the desired spot on the workpiece. The electromagnetic Deflector Coil then deflects this aligned stream (Beam) on to the work, through which the path of cut can be controlled. The Table, on which the workpiece is loaded, can also be traversed to feed the workpiece as needed. This high velocity beam of electrons impinges on the workpiece, where its Kinetic Energy is released and get converted into Heat Energy. The high intensity Heat, so produced, melts and vapourises the work material at the spot of beam impingement. By alternately focussing and turning off the beam, the cutting process can be continued as long as it is needed. Melting and vapourising of the metal takes only a Small Fraction of a Second and Turning off the beam is necessary to conduct away the heat from the workpiece. A suitable Viewing Device is always incorporated so as to enable the operator to observe the progress of machining operation.

Adequate vacuum is required to be maintained inside the chamber so that the Electrons can travel from cathode to anode without any Hinderence, there is not arc discharge between the electrodes, there is no loss of heat from the cathode, there is no contemination of the cathode and the High Velocity attained by the electron beam while leaving anode is maintained upto the event of its impingment on the work.

1.14.3 Process Capabilities and Limitations

(*a*) **Accuracy:** Tolerances are about 10% of the slot width or hole diameter. Taper of about 4° included angle is present in slots and holes. Heat affected zones of upto 0.03 mm deep have been observed. The stock removal rate is generally in the region of 1.5 mm^3/sec. with a penetration rate of about 0.25 mm/sec. or faster.

1.14.4 Advantages of E.B.M.

1. Any material can be machined.
2. workpiece is not subjected to any physical or metallurgical damage.
3. Problem of tool wear is non-existent. So, close dimensional tolerances can be achieved.
4. Heat can be concentrated on a particular spot.
5. An excellent technique for micro-machining.
6. There is no contact between the work and tool.
7. It can drill holes or cut slots which otherwise, cannot be made.
8. It is possible to cut any known material, metal or non-metal that can exist in vacuum.

1.14.5 Disadvantages of E.B.M.

1. High initial investment needed.
2. Highly skilled operator required to perform the operation.
3. Not suitable for producing perfectly cylindrical deep holes.
4. Suits for small and fine cuts only.
5. Workpiece size is limited due to requirement of vacuum in the chamber.
6. Low rate of metal removal.
7. High power consumptions.
8. Difficult to produce slots and holes of uniform shapes and dimensions.

1.14.6 Applications of E.B.M.

1. Very effective for machining of materials of low conductivity and high melting point.
2. Micro-machining operations on workpieces of thin sections.
3. Micro-drilling operations (upto 0.002 mm) for thin orifies, dies for wire drawing, parts of electron microscopes, fibre spinners, injector nozzles for diesel engines, etc.

QUESTIONS

1. What is Electric Discharge Machining (EDM)? Explain its principle with the help of a suitable diagram.
2. List the main Advantages and Disadvantages of EDM, and state few of its Industrial Applications.
3. Explain the function of Relaxation circuit in EDM.
4. What is Laser Beam Machining (LBM)? Explain its principle of operation with neat sketch.
5. What are the Advantages, Disadvantages and main Industrial Applications of LBM process?
6. Describe the principle of operation of Plasma Arc Machining (PAM) with neat sketch.
7. What are main Advantages, Disadvantages and Applications of PAM.
8. What is Electron Beam Machining (EBM)? Describe with neat sketch.
9. Describe Advantages, Diadvantages and main Applications of EBM.

REVIEW QUESTIONS

1. Explain the principle of Ultrasonic machining with the help of a neat diagram.
2. What are the main Advantages, Disadvantages and Applications of USM process?
3. Describe the mechanism of metal removal in USM and discuss the effects of the following parameters on metal removal: (*i*) Amplitude, (*ii*) Frequency (*iii*) Type of Abrasive, and (*iv*) Grain Size.
4. What is Abrasive Jet Machining (AJM) process? Explain its principles of operation.
5. What are main Advantages, Disadvantages, and Industrial Applications of AJM process?
6. What is Water Jet Machining (WJM) process? What are its main Applications?
7. Explain the principle of Hydrodynamic Jet Machining? How it differ's from WJM? What are its principle applications?
8. Explain the principle of Electrochemical Machining (ECM) Process.
9. What are main Advantages, Disadvantages and Applications of ECM?
10. With the help of neat diagram, explain the process of Electrochemical Grinding.
11. How does the metal removal take place in the Electrolytic Grinding both, by Abrasion and Chemical Deposition?
12. Describe the process of Chemical Machining (CHM), stating its main Advantages and Disadvantages.

13. What is Electric Discharge Machining (EDM)? Explain its principle with the help of a suitable diagram.
14. List the main Advantages and Disadvantages of EDM and state few of its Industrial Applications.
15. What is Laser Beam Machining (LBM)? Explain its principle of operation.
16. What are Advantages, Disadvantages and main Industrial Applications of LBM process?
17. What is Plasma Arc Machining (PAM)? Explain its principle of operation.
18. What are main Advantages, Disadvantages and Applications of PAM?
19. What is Electron Beam Machining (EBM), Describe with neat sketch.
20. Describe Advantages, Disadvantages and Applications of E.C.M.
21. How the Metal Removal and Feed Rates for Alloys can be calculated in ECM.
22. Discuss the main requirements of the Electrolyte and the Tool Material for use in ECM.
23. Explain the function of Relaxation circuit in EDM.

Chapter 2

Plastic Moulding Techniques

2.1 INTRODUCTION

Plastics are changed into useful shapes by using many different processes. The processes that are used to mould or shape thermoplastics basically soften the plastic material so it can be injected into a mould, flowed through a die, formed in or over a mould, etc. The processes usually allow any scrap parts or material to be ground up and reused. Some of the more common processes are injection moulding, extrusion, blow moulding, rotational moulding, calendering, thermoforming (which includes vacuum forming), compression moulding, transfer moulding and casting.

2.2 INJECTION MOULDING

"Injection Moulding" is used to make three dimensional shapes with great detail. It is a fast process and is used to produce large numbers of identical items from high precision engineering components to disposable consumer goods. It is the process that moulds plastic through heat and pressure, by injecting molten plastic polymer into the desired mould.

Materials such as Acrylonitrile-Butadiene-Styrene (ABS), polystyrene, nylon, polypropylene and polythene can be used in this process. These are thermoplastics—this means when they are heated and then pressured in a mould they can be formed into different shapes. A simple diagram of an injection moulding machine is shown in the Fig. 2.1.

The mould on this machine has been made to form plastic into a sphere.

1. Granules of plastic powder are poured or fed into a hopper which stores it until it is needed.
2. A heater heats up the tube and when it reaches a high temperature a screw thread starts turning.
3. A motor turns a thread which pushes the granules along the heater section which melts them into a liquid.
4. The liquid is forced into a mould where it cools into the shape (in this case a sphere).
5. The mould then opens and the sphere is removed.
6. The mould is then closed and ready for the next shot.

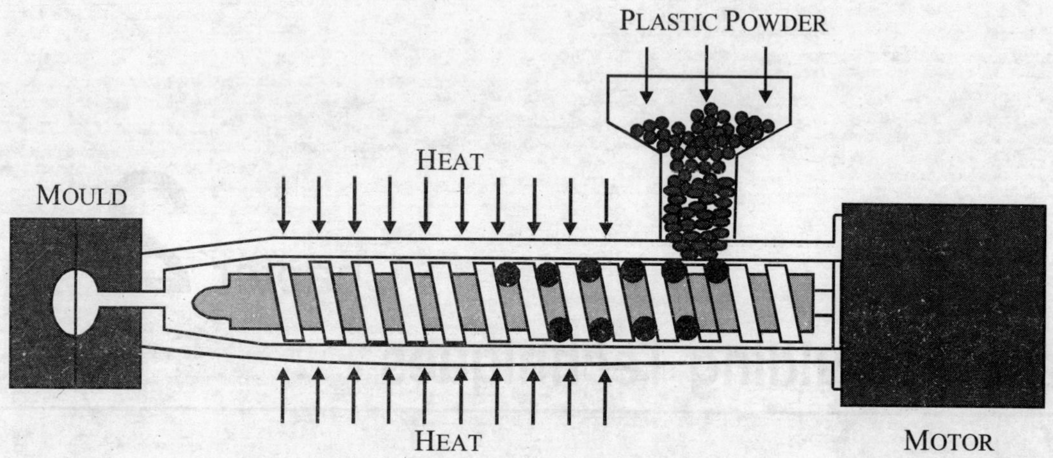

Fig. 2.1: Injection Moulding Machine.

The moulds are most often made out of hardened steel and carefully finished. They may also be made out of prehard steel, aluminum, epoxy, etc. The type of mould material selected depends on the number of parts to be made and the plastic material to be used. Parts are often machined to test the shape and function of a part before a mould is built.

Injection moulding is predominately used for thermoplastics but smaller amounts of thermosets and elastomers are also processed this way. The injection moulding of thermosets is similar to the injection moulding of thermoplastics except the material is kept cool until it is pushed into the heated mould where it is crosslinked. The mould is then opened and the hot, but rigid, part is removed.

Advantages of injection moulding are-

1. It gives a good surface finish.
2. Can be used for very complex mouldings.
3. Economically viable in mass production and gives a very low unit production cost.

Applications include computer enclosures, milk crates, CD cases, mobile phones, power-tool housings, safety helmets, telephone handsets, television cabinets, washing-up bowls, butter tubs, yogurt containers, closures, fittings and razors.

2.2.1 Reaction Injection Moulding

This process is similar to injection moulding except that normally thermosetting plastics are used. Often foamed parts with solid skin are produced.

In reaction injection moulding two or more kinds of fluid plastics are mixed, often without being heated, and then injected into a mould where the mixture solidifies. A simple diagram of a reaction injection moulding machine is shown in the Fig. 2.2. Stiffness of the parts produced by this process can be increased using different kinds of fibre reinforcement. An advantage of this process is that moulding costs are relatively low.

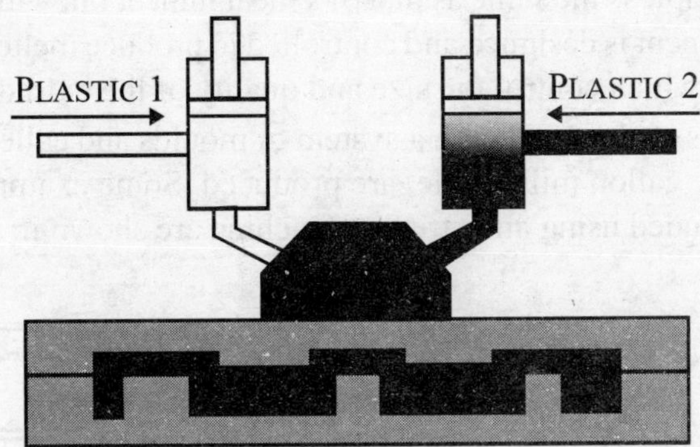

Fig. 2.2: Reaction Injection Moulding Machine.

Applications include automobile bumper, panton chair and shoe soles.

2.3 EXTRUSION

"Extrusion" is like squeezing toothpaste out of its tube. This continuous process is used for the production of semi-finished goods such as films, sheet profiles, tubs and pipes. They are termed "semi-finished" because they must be further processed before they become useful articles. A machine used to extrude materials is very similar to the injection moulding machine described in the previous article. Plastic material is first loaded into a hopper and then fed into a long heated chamber through which it is moved by the action of a continuously revolving screw. At the end of the heated chamber, the molten plastic is forced out through a small opening called a die that is cast in the shape of the finished product. As the plastic extrusion comes from the die, it is fed onto a conveyor belt where it is cooled by blowers or by immersion in water. A simple diagram of an extrusion machine is shown in the Fig. 2.3.

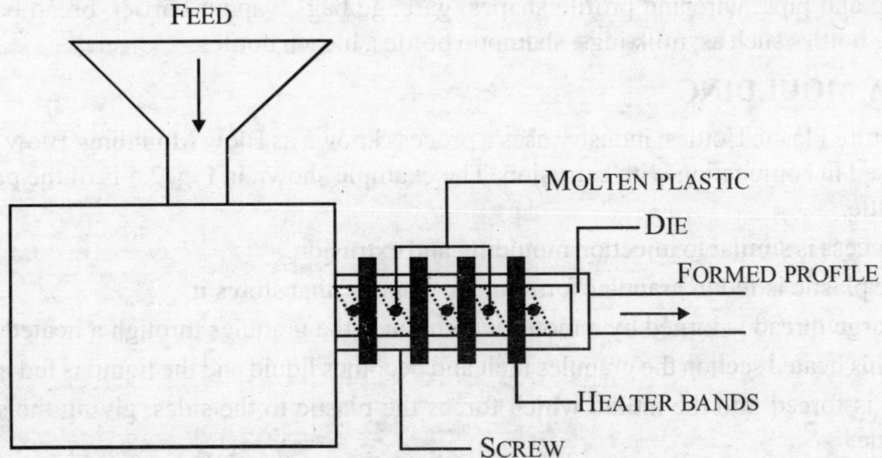

Fig. 2.3: Extrusion Machine.

The operation's principle is the same as that of a meat mincer but with added heaters in the wall of the extruder. The equipment is designed and controlled to produce melted plastic at a very uniform temperature and pressure which control the size and quality of the extruded product.

The extrusion process is also used with a system of moulds and called "Blow Moulding." This is how bottles, such as the gallon milk bottle, are produced. Some examples of the type of .shapes (sections) that can be extruded using an extrusion machine are shown in Fig. 2.4.

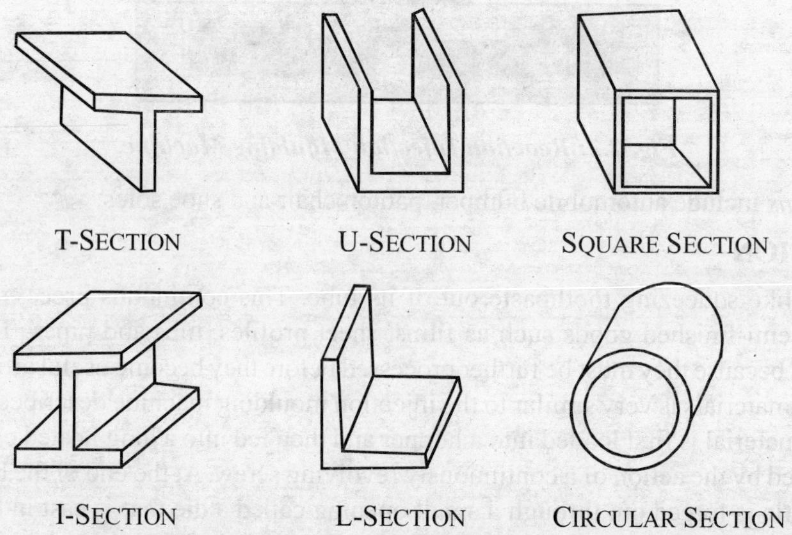

Fig. 2.4: Examples of the Type of Shapes (Sections) that can be Extruded.

Applications include drinking straws, decorative moulding, window trimming, plastic tube, sheet, lawn edging and pipe, wire and profile shapes, garbage bags, vapour barrier, bread bags, grocery bags, plastic bottles such as; milk jugs, shampoo bottles, bleach bottles.

2.4 BLOW MOULDING

To manufacture Plastic Bottles, industry uses a process known as Blow Moulding. Blow moulding is a process used in conjunction with extrusion. The example shown in Fig. 2.5 is of the production of a plastic bottle.

The process is similar to injection moulding and extrusion.

1. The plastic is fed in granular form into a 'hopper' that stores it.
2. A large thread is turned by a motor which feeds the granules through a heated section.
3. In this heated section the granules melt and becomes liquid and the liquid is fed into a mould.
4. Air is forced into the mould which forces the plastic to the sides, giving the shape of the bottle.
5. The mould is then cooled and is removed.

6. The bottle may they be conveyed on to trimming, printing and filling stations.

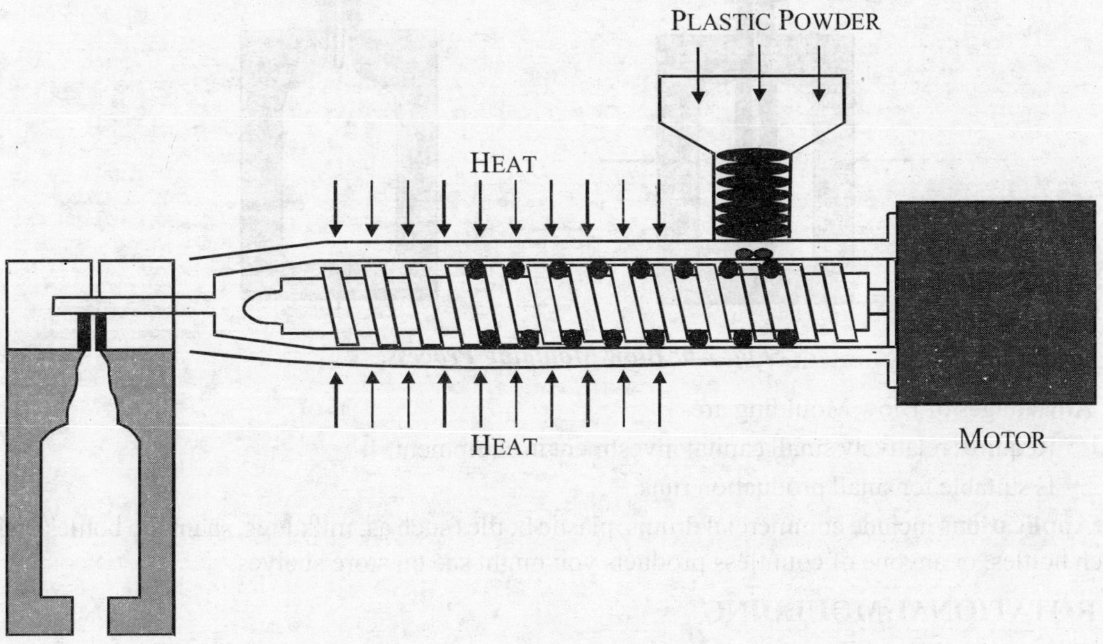

Fig. 2.5: Blow Moulding Machine.

Overall, the goal is to produce a uniform melt, form it into a tube with the desired cross-section and blow it into the exact shape of the product as shown in Fig. 2.6. This process is intended for use in manufacturing hollow plastic products and its principal advantage is its ability to produce hollow shapes without having to join two or more separately moulded parts. Extrusion blow moulding can be used to process many different plastics, including HOPE, PVC, PC, PP and PETG. Other processes for Blow Moulding include Stretch Blow and Injection Blow.

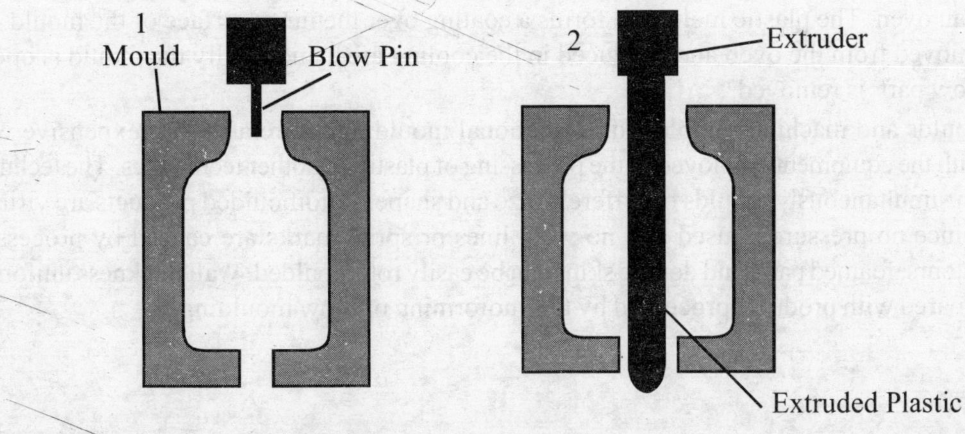

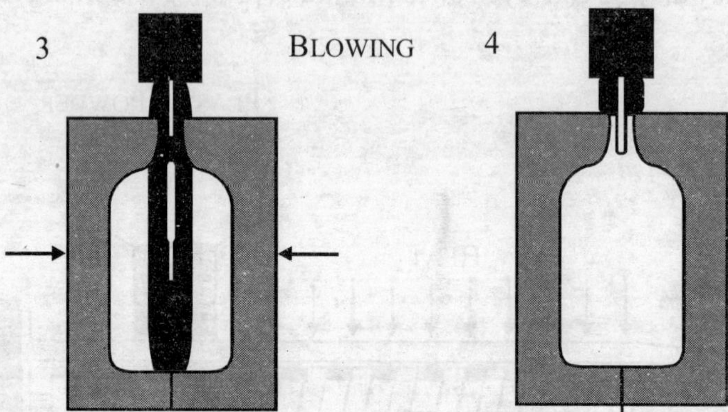

Fig. 2.6: Blow Moulding Process.

Advantages of Blow Moulding are-

1. Requires relatively small capital investment in equipment.
2. Is suitable for small production runs.

Applications include commercial drums, plastic bottles such as; milk jugs, shampoo bottles and bleach bottles, or anyone of countless products you might see on store shelves.

2.5 ROTATIONAL MOULDING

Rotational moulding is a technique for the transformation of plastics in hollow articles such as doll's heads, tanks, containers, gloves, etc. The technique allows to obtain small parts of a few grams as well as containers of more than 20000 litres of capacity. Foamed parts, multi-layer mouldings or soft mouldings without joining lines can also be produced, which gives an idea of the versatility of this technique. Inversions and costs of production are very low when compared with other plastics processing techniques as injection moulding or blow moulding. The process may use fluoropolymers and thermoplastics, such as : low density polyethylene (LDPE), polypropylene (PP), ethylene vinyl acetate (EVA) and polyvinyl chloride (PYC).

The rotational moulding process consists of four steps as illustrated in Fig. 2.7. A given amount of plastic, either, in powder or liquid form, is deposited in a mould. After closing the mould, it rotate biaxially in an oven. The plastic melts and forms a coating over the inner surface of the mould. The mould is removed from the oven and produced in the cooling area, and finally the mould is opened and the hollow part is removed.

The moulds and machines employed in rotational moulding are relatively inexpensive when compared with the equipment employed in the processing of plastics by other techniques. The technique allows to run simultaneously moulds of different size and shape. Rotomoulded products are virtually stress-free since no pressure is used and no weld lines or sprue marks are caused by processing. Intricate contours, foamed parts and double skins can be easily rotomoulded. Wall thickness uniformity is good compared with products processed by thermoforming or blow moulding.

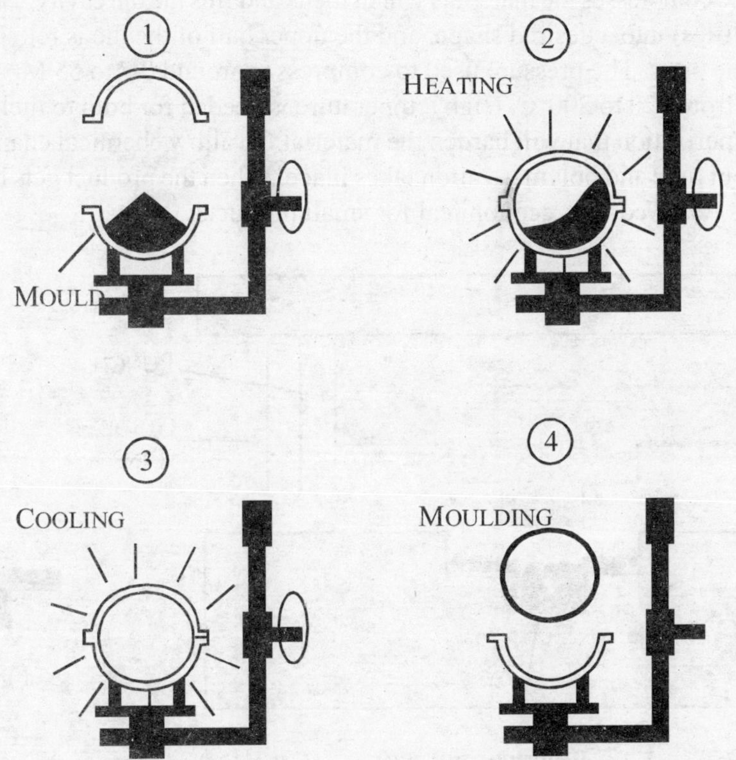

Fig. 2.7: Rotational Moulding Process.

There are some problems associated with the moulding obtained by this process if precautions are not taken. Porosity and bubbles content, thickness distribution, pigments distribution, cycle time, warpage or shrinkage can be important depending on the flow capacity of the material selected, heating rate, cooling rate, mould material and rotation rate. All these variables must be carefully selected in order to avoid the mentioned problems. Parts with special features also required a study prior to production.

Applications of Rotational Moulding are-

1. Toy industry—Dolls, play balls, bicycles, riding cars, wading pools, picnic tables, riding horses, etc.
2. Industry, transportation—Tanks and containers for many applications.
3. Recreational area—Boats, kayaks, playground equipment.
4. Specials applications—Planter pots, accessories, furnitures.

2.6 COMPRESSION MOULDING

Compression moulding is a process in which a powder or granular form of thermosetting materials are compressed into a desired shape. The compression moulding process is shown in Fig. 2.8. The upper half of the die compresses the materials which melts and fills the die cavity. The part polymerizes or cures (*i.e.* solidifies) into a desired shape, and the upper half of the die is retracted and opened in order to remove the parts. The pressure used to compress is around 0.7 to 55 Mpa. The temperature used is anywhere from 120 to 200°C. High temperature is needed for both to melt the raw materials and to cause polymerization that will harden the material. To allow chemical changes, mould is kept closed for sufficient time and polymerization takes place. When the product gets hardened, mould is opened and part is removed. It is economical for small products.

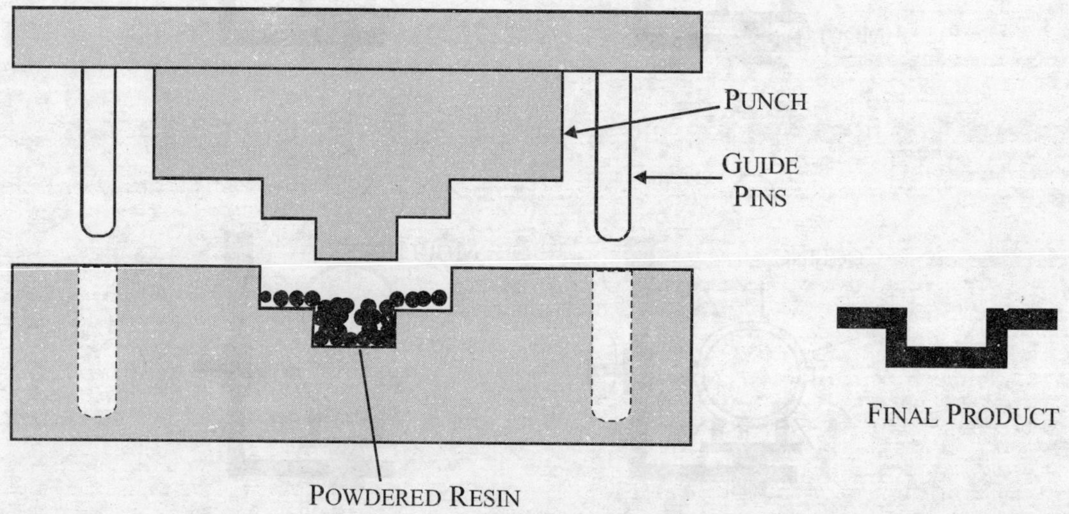

Fig. 2.8: Compression Moulding.

Applications include electrical switch, fuse boxes, domestic electrical equipment, microwave containers, gas and electricity meter, housing and dish aerials.

2.7 TRANSFER MOULDING

Transfer moulding is a process in which heat and pressure are used to transfer partially melted thermoplastics into the cavity with a sprue. After the thermoplastic is cured inside the cavity, it is then removed. The differences between the compression moulding and that of transfer moulding is that the curing time for the latter is usually less than the former. The loading time is also shorter. Transfer moulding is usually the preferred method for producing parts that have a large variation in section thickness. However, the cost of die and sprue could make this method more expensive than compression moulding. Fig. 2.9 shows a cross-section view of the transfer moulding machine.

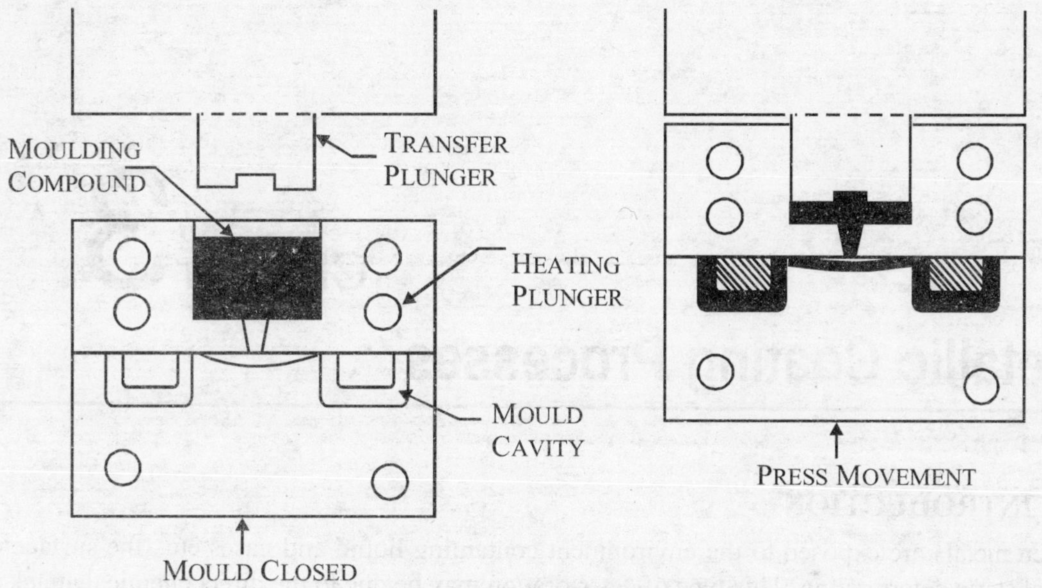

Fig. 2.9: Transfer Moulding Machine.

REVIEW QUESTIONS

1. Describe the process of injection moulding with the help of neat sketch.
2. With the help of neat sketch, describe the process of compression moulding.
3. What advantages does injection moulding have over compression moulding?
4. With the help of neat sketches, describe the process of making plastic bottles.
5. Describe with neat sketches, the following processes, stalting their advantages and applications:
   (*i*) Compression moulding, and
   (*ii*) Blow moulding

Chapter 3

Metallic Coating Processes

3.1 INTRODUCTION

When metals are exposed to the environment containing liquid and gases etc., the surface of the metal starts deteriorating. This type of deterioration may be due to the direct chemical attack and is known as corrosion. There are many examples of corrosion in day-to-day life, but the two most familiar examples are the rusting of iron and the formation of green film on the surface of copper. The rusting of iron takes place, when the iron is exposed to atmospheric conditions. During this exposure, a layer of reddish scale and powder of oxide is formed and the iron becomes weak. The formation of green film on the surface of copper takes place when it is exposed to moist air containing carbon dioxide.

Thus, it is very necessary to prevent or reduce the rate of corrosion. For this, a protective coating is applied on the base metal. The protective coatings may be broadly classified into the following two categories:

1. Metallic coating, and
2. Non-metallic (organic or inorganic) coating.

These coatings are also done for better appearance and decorative purposes.

3.2 CLEANING OF METALS

Before metallic or non-metallic coating is applied, the first step is to clean the surface of the base metal, in order to provide good adhesion and finish. There are many types of contaminants such as dirt, oil, grease, oxide, scale etc., which ultimately affect the life of the product. The selection of a cleaning process mainly depends upon the type of contaminants, degree of cleanliness required and the composition of the metal. The cleaning may be done by chemical methods or by mechanical methods as discussed in the following pages.

3.3 CHEMICAL METHODS OF CLEANING

The cleaning of metals by chemical methods may be done by alkalines, acids and solvents. Some of the chemical cleaning methods are described below:

1. **Alkaline Cleaning:** The alkaline cleaning is most efficient and economical in removing oil and grease by saponification or emulsification or both. The alkaline cleaners are prepared from cleaning agents such as caustic soda or sodium metasilicate which are added to some type of soap to aid in emulsification. The common methods of applying alkaline cleaners include electro cleaning, spray cleaning, dip-tank cleaning and steam cleaning. After cleaning, the parts must be thoroughly rinsed with water, otherwise, any trace of alkali, left on the surface of metal, may corrode it.

   The alkaline cleaners are used on all metals except zinc, lead, tin, brass and aluminium as these metals are chemically active and may be attacked by alkaline cleaners.

2. **Acid Pickling:** The acid pickling is the most common method of removing oxide scale or flux residue from the surface of metals. Before this process is done, alkaline cleaning of part is done to remove dirt, greases and oils in order to obtain an even removal of oxides during the pickling process. In this method, either diluted sulphuric acid, hydrochloric acid, phosphoric acid or muriatic acid is sprayed on the part or the part is dipped in a tank, agitated and then washed and rinsed thoroughly. It may be noted that sulphuric acid and the muriatic acid solutions can be used while hot, but the hydrochloric acid solution is used at room temperature. The acid pickling is used for removing oil and grease. In some cases, it is used for removing light rust.

3. **Solvent Cleaning:** The solvent cleaning is primarily used to remove oil, grease and dirt on metals such as zinc, lead and aluminium. It may be performed by either emulsified solvent or chlorinated solvent. In *emulsified solvent cleaning process*, an organic solvent is mixed with a hydrocarbon-soluble emulsifying agent (i.e., soap and kerosene mixture with a small amount of water). The cleaning is done by dipping the part in the solution and then rinsed. To remove heavy oil or dirt, the part is stirred in a tank or sprayed with hot solution, and then rinsed. The parts which needs to be electroplated afterwards must be treated with alkaline cleaner to remove any organic matter left on the surface.

   The *chlorinated solvent cleaning* (also known as vapour degreasing) is an effective and widely used method of removing heavy oils and greases. This method provides a high degree of surface cleanliness. In this method, either a solution of trichloroethylene (boiling point 85°C), or perchloro-ethylene (boiling point 120°C) is heated in a tank to its boiling point and the vapours are produced. The parts placed in a wire basket are suspended in these vapours. This causes the vapours to condense on the metal surfaces and removes all the oil and grease. The disadvantage of this method is that the vapours do not remove the solid dirt and the organic matter, hence vapour degreasing is followed by alkaline cleaning.

3.4 MECHANICAL METHODS OF CLEANING

The cleaning of metals by mechanical methods may be performed as discussed below:

1. **Abrasive Blast Cleaning:** The abrasive blast cleaning is widely used for removing all classes of scale and rust from forgings, castings, weldments and heat-treated parts. Cleaning is done either in dry or wet abrasive blasting machines. The abrasive blast cleaning equipment

consists of cleaning cabinet, an abrasive reserviour and an air nozzle. The abrasive particles such as sand, steel grit or shot are drawn through the hose to join the high velocity air stream at the nozzle and strike against the surface of the metal to be cleaned. The used abrasives slides down the centrally sloped bottom of the cabinet and return to the reservoir.

In case of wet abrasive blasting machines, the wet abrasive slurry is fed into the blasting gun by a centrifugal pump, which forces it to exit through the nozzle along with compressed air. Silica, soft silicon dioxide, quartz or aluminium oxide are used as wet abrasives.

2. **Tumbling:** The tumbling in dry abrasive is used for removing rust and scale from small metal parts of simple shape. In this method, the workpieces are placed in a drum along with abrasive materials. The abrasive materials can be granite chips, aluminium oxide pellets or sand. In operation, the drum is rotated and the movement of the workpieces and the abrasive materials against each other produces by friction a fine cutting action, which removes rust and scale from the product.

   Tumbling is the least expensive cleaning method. However, parts with complex shape, deep recess and other irregularities cannot be descaled uniformly by tumbling. It may require several hours of tumbling to complete the cleaning, but if slugs of various sizes and shapes are mixed, good results can be achieved. Slug reaches all corners and cavities and clean it. It may be noted that by this process cleaning is not possible. The entire surface of the part is subjected to cleaning during this process.

3. **Barrel Rolling:** Barrel rolling and tumbling are principally the same processes with the only difference that in former process barrel is loaded about 40 to 60 percent capacity, while in tumbling it is nearly full.

   The abrasives used in this are slag, cinders, sharp sand, granite chips, silicon carbide or aluminium oxide along with water, dilute acid or soap solution. Sometimes, scrap punching or mineral matter is also added for wet rolling. For dry rolling, hard wood dust or leather scrap is added to keep workpieces separate from each other.

   In operation, as the barrel rotates, the parts roll over and falls to the bottom of the barrel. This motion cuts down the surface of parts.

4. **Power Brushing:** Power brushing is used to remove light rust, heat treatment scale, weld flux, machining burns and other unwanted contaminants. One of the major advantage of powerbrush is that it can be used in manual, semi-automatic or integrated methods.

   In manual brushing, the part is fed against a rotating wheel brush by hand whereas in automatic machines, parts move past a series of rotating brushes, removing very little metal. When the brushes are used with fine abrasive compounds, they can produce fine finish on metal surfaces.

   The selection of the brush is based upon the surface to be cleaned. Wire wheel brushes made of steel, brass and stainless steel are used to remove contaminants from nickel alloys, brass alloys, copper, bronze, brass, steel and stainless steel parts.

5. **Buffing and Polishing:** The basic purpose of buffing and polishing operation is to obtain highly reflective and polished surfaces. However, buffing produces a relatively more reflective, smooth, uniform surface with a high brilliant lustre as compared to polishing. The buffing

wheels are made from very soft materials like felt, muslin or linen and are made in 'Various forms like radial, parallel, concentric, square etc. The abrasive used for buffing is a very fine powder of crushed flint, quartz, silicon carbide, aluminium oxide and iron oxide (red-rouge). To reduce abrading or roughing action, the abrasive is blended with some lubricant like grease, wax, glue, oil or tallon, to give a flowing action.

The polishIng process involves the use of dry abrasive in oil or some other lubricant. Generally, the polishing wheels are made from canvas muslin, felt and leather. As a result of polishing operation, the surface layer of the metal is locally plastically deformed, due to which the surface inequalities are removed, scratches are finished and compressive residual stresses are induced in the metal. Consequently the fatigue resistance of the parts is increased in addition to obtaining a highly reflective surface.

In both buffing and polishing operations, workpiece is held in fixtures, on a rotating circular work table. The table moves past a series of adjustable polishing and buffing wheels. The wheels are adjusted, according to the shape of the workpiece, to polish all its surfaces. Sometimes the polishing and buffing wheels are mounted on floor polishing lathes for ordinary finish.

3.5 METALLIC COATINGS

These are the coatings of metals, which are applied on the base metal to prevent corrosion as well as for decorative purposes. The metallic coatings may be obtained by the following methods:

1. Hot dipping,
2. Electroplating,
3. Metal spraying,
4. Metal cladding, and
5. Cementation.

The methods are discussed, in detail, in the following pages.

3.6 HOT DIPPING

It is mainly used to apply coatings of low melting metals such as zinc, tin, cadmium, aluminium or, lead on iron, steel and copper which have relatively higher melting temperatures. In this method, the article is cleaned and dipped in a bath of molten metal. It is then taken out from the bath and finished properly. The most common processes of hot dipping are galvanising and tin plating as discussed below:

1. **Galvanising:** It is a process of providing thin layer of zinc coating (highly corrosion resistant) on iron or low carbon steel by dipping them in a bath of molten zinc. It improves the resistance against corrosion due to atmosphere and water. Since zinc is anodic to iron or steel (which serves as cathodic), therefore the zinc coating (also called anodic coating) is obtained by electrochemical reaction between the zinc and the iron or steel. The process is carried out as follows:

   First of all, the work is cleaned by pickling with dilute sulphuric acid, to remove any scale, rust and impurities. After washing and drying, it is dipped in a bath of molten zinc maintained at a temperature of about 450°C. The surface of the bath is kept covered with a molten flux layer usually of zinc ammonium chloride to prevent oxide formation. The duration of immersion in a zinc bath depends upon the size of the work to be coated. It is then taken out from the bath and passed through a pair of rollers to remove any excess of zinc. Finally, the work is cooled and dried.

The galvanising process is widely used for sheetings for roofs and walls of building, structural parts, pipes, containers, fencing materials, nails, wires etc.

2. **Tin Plating or Tinning:** It is a process of providing a thin layer of tin coating on the iron or steel sheets. In this process, the metal sheet is first treated with dilute sulphuric acid (pickling) to remove any oxide film. It is then fluxed by passing through a bath of zinc chloride. The flux helps the molten tin to adhere to the metal sheet. Now the sheet is dipped into a tank of molten tin which is maintained at a temperature of approximately 320°C. This process gives a coating thickness of about 0.003 mm. Finally, the sheet is passed through a series of rollers to remove any excess of tin and produce a thin layer of uniform thickness on the sheet.

   The tin plating or tinning is generally done on metal sheets used for manufacturing containers for storing foodstuffs, ghee, oils, kerosene and packing food materials. The tinned-copper sheets are employed for making cooking utensils and refrigeration equipments.

3.7 ELECTROPLATING

It is the process of depositing a very thin layer of metal coating, on the base metal, by passing a direct current through an electrolyte solution containing some salt of the coating metal. Now-a-days, the electroplating is one of the best methods for the commercial production of a metallic coating.

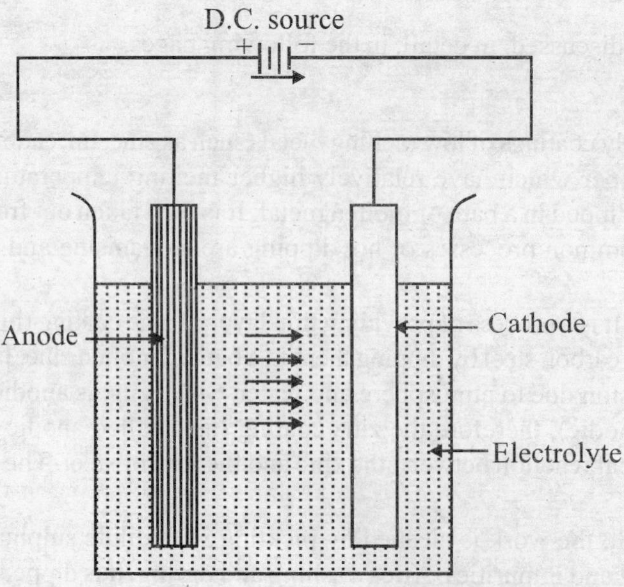

Fig. 3.1: Electroplating

In this process, the article to be electroplated is first immersed in hot alkaline solution to remove oil and grease. It is then treated with dilute hydrochloric acid or sulphuric acid to remove scale and oxides. It may be noted that hydrochloric acid is used for nickel and copper plating, while sulphuric acid is used for chromium plating. The cleaned article is made to act as cathode whereas the coating metal as an anode. The cathode and anode are dipped in a solution containing some salt of the coating material *i.e.*, electrolyte, as shown in Fig. 3.1. When direct current is passed, the coating metal ions migrate to the cathode and get deposited there. Thus a thin layer of coating metal is obtained on the article, which is made as cathode. The thickness of coating can be 0.005 mm or more. The commonly used metals, which are used for electroplating, are copper, nickel, chromium, silver, gold, cadmium and tungsten.

The electroplating is extensively used for decorative purposes and for protecting iron and steel articles from corrosion.

3.8 METAL SPRAYING

It is a process of providing a thin coating by depositing an atomized metal on the surface of the base metal. In this process, the coating metal in the molten state is sprayed on the prepared surface of the base metal. Following are the two common methods of metal spraying:

1. **Wire Gun Method:** In this method, the coating metal in the wire from is sprayed from a gun torch, as shown in Fig. 3.2.

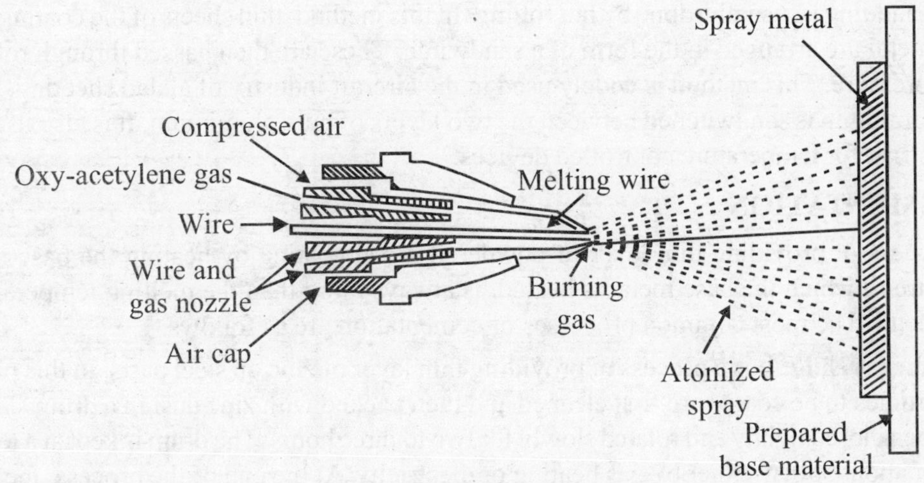

Fig. 3.2: Metal Spraying

The wire is drawn through the gun and nozzle by a pair of rollers and melted by an oxy-acetylene flame. A blast of compressed air is used to atomize the molten metal and deposit it uniformly on the prepared surface. Though any metal that can be drawn into wire, can be used in this gun but the mostly used are alloys such as steel, bronze, aluminium and nickel.

2. **Powder Metal Method:** This method is also known as thermospray method. In this method, the coating metal in the finely divided powdered form is fed from a container through a rubber hose to the spray gun. The powdered metal gets melted almost instantly as it passes through the oxy-acetylene or hydrogen gas flame. In this, no compressed air is required as there is sufficient force of the gas flame to carry the atomized metal at high speed to the surface being sprayed. This method is, however, limited to low melting metals like zinc, lead, tin etc.

The metal spraying method has the following advantages over other coating methods :

1. The coating can be applied to large and irregularly shaped objects.
2. The coating can be applied to fabricated structure and there is no possibility of damage to the coating.
3. The coating can be applied even on to non-metallic objects made of glass, wood, plastic etc.

3.9 METAL CLADDING

It is a process of providing a comparatively thicker layer of coating on the metal surface. The main object of cladding is to produce a corrosion resistant surface. All the corrosion resisting metals (like nickel, copper, lead, silver etc.) and alloys (like stainless steel, nickel alloys, copper alloys, lead alloys etc.) can be used as cladding material. The base metal on which cladding is done are mild steel, aluminium, copper, nickel and their alloys.

The cladding is, usually, done by hot rolling. In this method, thin sheets of the coating metal and the base metal are arranged in the form of a sandwich. These are then passed through rollers under heat and pressure. This method is widely used in the aircraft industry of alclad sheeting, in which a plate of duralumin is sandwitched between the two layers of pure aluminium. It is also used to make bi-metal strips for temperature controlled devices.

3.10 CEMENTATION

It is a process of providing thin layer of powdered metal coating by heating the base metal. The temperature to which the base metal is heated, is always more than the melting temperature of the coating metal. The most common processes of cementation are as follows:

1. **Sheradising:** It is a process of providing thin layer of zinc on steel parts. In this process, the articles to be coated are first cleaned and then packed with zinc dust in a drum. The drum is then closed tightly and rotated slowly for two to three hours. The drum is kept at a temperature of about 350°C either by gas heating or electricity. At the end of the process, the surface of the articles are covered with a thin layer of zinc.

   The sheradising improves the resistance against corrosion. It is used especially for small steel articles such as bolts, screws, nuts, washers, etc.
2. **Chromizing:** It is a process of providing thin layer of chromium on steel parts. This process is carried out by heating chromium powder (55%) and alumina (45%) with the steel parts at about 1300 – 1400°C for 3 to 4 hours. The alumina is used to prevent coalescence of chromium particles.

The chromizing greatly improves the resistance against oxidation. It is extensively applied for turbine blades.

3. **Calorizing:** It is process of providing thin layer of aluminium on steel parts. In this process, the steel parts are first cleaned by sand blasting and then heated in a tightly packed drum with a mixture of aluminium powder and aluminium oxide together with a small quantity of ammonium chloride as a flux. The process is carried out in a reducing atmosphere of hydrogen at 900°c for 24 hrs. Upon heating, the aluminium diffuses deeper into the metal and the coating becomes thicker but it may be noted that because of diffusion the average aluminium content is lower.

The calorizing improves the resistance to oxidation at high temperatures. It is very suitable for treating steel parts for furnaces, oil refineries, driers and kilns etc.

3.11 ANODIZING

It is a process by which an oxide film is deposited on a metal surface, for providing corrosion resistant and decorative finish. Generally, aluminium and its alloys are anodized since aluminium has a natural tendency to get oxidised when exposed to atmosphere but anodizing can also be done on metals like lead, magnesium, copper, zinc, bronze etc.

An electrolytic circuit is used in the process, in which the workpiece is made an anode. The electrolyte which is generally aqueous solution of sulphuric acid, oxalic acid and chromic acid which give up oxygen on electrolysis. Lead or graphite is made as cathode. When a direct current (D.C.) is passed through the electrolyte, oxygen is liberated at the surface of the anode, which impinges on the workpiece, forming a porous oxide film, giving it cellular structure appearance. It may be noted that to close the pores, the oxide film is further subjected to a process called *sealing*, in order to make it permanent and durable. This can be done by treating the oxide film with boiling water-steam bath (85°C to 100°C) or dilute nickel acetate solution. The coating produced by this method have greyish green colour. Other colours can also be obtained by using a suitable dye material.

The thickness and density of the oxide layer depends on the anodizing conditions and on the conditions of the metal being anodized. The higher the proportion of acid in the solution, the thicker will be the anodized film but the film be porous and soft. The film thickness also increases with current density, the anodizing time and with the lowering of the temperature of the solution. Also, an alternating current produces a thin anodizing layer whereas a direct current produce a coating, having deeper penetration.

The anodized metal can be directly used for drawing and forming operations, without destroying the coating or its protective qualities, as the coating is an integral part of the metal. Aircraft materials, gift wares, home appliances, hardware, aluminium door frames, channels, etc., are anodized by this process.

3.12 NON-METALLIC COATINGS

These are the coatings of non-metals, which are applied on the base metal. Following are the various types of non-metallic coatings:

1. Paints,
2. Varnishes,
3. Lacquers,
4. Enamels,
5. Plastic coatings,
6. Chemical coatings,
7. Vitreous enamel coatings, and
8. Ceramic coatings.

These are discussed, in detail, in the following pages.

3.13 PAINTS

The paints are fluids designed to cover the materials (like steel plates, resin etc.) to be coated with coating film which protects them and improves their appearance. In general, following are the purposes of applying a paint:

1. **Protection of the object:** The paints are rust proof, corrosion proof and have good resistance against oil, weather and shock.
2. **Appearance of the object:** The paints have good colour, high gloss, smoothness and cubic effect.
3. **Others:** The paints have good sound proof properties.

The paint commonly used for engineering purposes is an oil paint. It is a fluid paste prepared by dissolving a base into a vehicle along with a colouring pigment. The bases used in oil paints are white lead, zinc white, red lead etc., and the vehicles are linseed oil, poppy oil, nut oil, tung oil etc. The colouring pigments include black, blue, brown etc. The other ingredients of an oil paint are solvent or thinner, drier and inert filler. The solvent or thinner (turpentine oil, petroleum, spirit, etc.) is used to modify the consistency of the paint. The drier (litharge, lead acetate, manganese sulphate etc.) enables the paint to dry quickly. The inert filler (powdered chalk, charcoal, silica etc.) are used to make the paint economical and of desired quality.

Before applying a coat of paint, the primer (lead oxide) has to be applied first to the surface, in order to secure proper cohesion of the paint. When a thin coating is applied on any surface, the thinner evaporates from the painted surface and the drying oil gets oxidised, thus forming a dry thin pigmented film.

A large number of ready made paints are available in the market under various trade marks. These paints are usually too thick to be applied in a thin uniform layer. They are, therefore, made thin by adding a suitable quantity of oil while using them. The paint may be applied either by a brush, spray gun or dipping. The spraying with a spray gun is rapid and gives a smooth painted surface.

3.14 VARNISHES

The varnish is a homogeneous mixture of natural or synthetic resin in a particular solvent. The commonly used resins are copal, amber, lac or shellac, dammer etc., and the solvents are linseed oil, turpentine oil, methylated spirit or alcohol. A drier (litharge) is also added to help in quick drying of varnish.

The varnish is used as a protective and decorative coating of suitable surfaces. When it dries, it leaves a hard, transparent, glossy, lustrous and durable film. The following are the main two types of varnishes:

1. Oil varnishes, and 2. Spirit varnishes.

The *oil varnish* is a homgeneous solution of one or more resins in a drying oil (linseed oil) and a volatile solvent (turpentine oil) and drier. This type of varnish takes longer period for drying, but the film produced is hard, quite lustrous and durable.

The *spirit varnish* is obtained by dissolving the resin (lac or shallac) in a volatile solvent (methylated spirit). This type of varnish dries quite rapidly, but the film produced is brittle and thus, has the tendancy to crack or peel off. Such varnishes are used, usually, for polishing wooden surfaces.

3.15 LACQUERS

The lacquer is a solution made by dissolving nitrocellulose, resin and plasticizer in a solvent with or without the colouring pigments. In a lacquer, nitrocellulose provides toughness and resistance to abrasion; the resins (such as alkyd, copal, dammer, ester, gum etc.) increase adhesion and hardness and the plasticizer (castor oil) is added to improve elasticity and plasticity. The solvent is usually a mixture of ketone, alcohol and a hydrocarbon.

Since the lacquer has quick drying property due to the evaporation of solvent, therefore it is widely used for giving a finish to automobile bodies. It is also used for preparing artificial leather and for painting of interior wood work, metal surfaces, furniture etc. for decoration purposes.

3.16 ENAMELS

The enamel is a pigmented varnish which dry into a very lustrous and glossy finish, having very good flow. In other words, it is an intimate dispersion of pigment in a varnish. The properties of an enamel depends largely upon the varnish's vehicle and resin. The following two types of enamels are available, depending upon the method of drying used:

1. Air-drying enamel, and 2. Baking enamel.

When enamel dries at room temperature by oxidation or polymerization or by both, it is then known as air-drying enamel.

When enamel dries at elevated temperature either in the presence or absence of oxygen, it is then known as baking enamel. It provides a hard and more abrasive resistant finish than air drying enamel.

It may be noted that the drying process mainly depends upon the purpose for which the product is finally used. The enamels are available in all colours and can be applied easily. They have the ability to resist corrosive atmospheres and attack of most chemical agents. These are mostly used in metal processing industry.

3.17 PLASTIC COATINGS

The plastic coatings have good resistance to corrosion, good adhesion ability, high resistance to abrasion and attractive appearance. The plastic coated metals are used in chemical plant equipments, tank, pipe lines, valve bodies, water treatment plants etc. Following plastics are generally used for coating purposes:

1. Plasticized polyvinyl chloride (P.V.C); 2. Nylon;

3. Penton;
4. Cellulose acetate butyrate (C.A.B);
5. polyethylene (Polythene);
6. Polytetra fluro ethylene (P.T.F.E.);
7. Polytrifluro monochloro ethylene (P.T.F.C.E.);
8. Polyester/Polymethane;
9. Polypropylene; and
10. Acrylics.

The various methods of coating the plastics on metals are discussed below:

1. **Fine Powder Dipping:** In this method, the hot Parts are dipped into a gas agitated bed of fine powder. The part is further heated to fuse the coated particles so that a smooth film is formed on the part. By this method, polyethylene, P.V.C., nylon or C.A.B. are coated on various metals.
2. **Liquid Plastisol Method (Dip Coating):** In this method, the hot parts are dipped in a liquid plastisol tank. The plastisol will form a gelled coating on the part. The coating thickness upto 12mm can be achieved by this method. Generally electrical parts, tool handles, automotive bumpers, plate and dish racks are coated by this process.
3. **Electrostatic Spraying:** The electrostatic spray method consists of a powder reservoir or hopper, powder feed mechanism, a spraying gun and a generator. The powder is fed to the gun by means of an air pump. The spray gun is applied with high voltage source so that the particles impelled at high velocity gets strongly charged. The part which is to be coated is earthed, therefore charged particles are attracted toward the part thus forming a layer on the part.
4. **Vacuum Coating:** In this method, vacuum is used to attract the powder on the surface of a preheated part. No air is entrapped in coating as the process is done in absence of air. Generally nylon and penton are coated by this method.

3.18 CHEMICAL COATINGS

In this process, the metal to be coated is cleaned and dipped in a chemical solution in the same way as the plastic coating. The chemical solution is, generally, prepared by dissolving a metal having higher resistance against corrosion in some suitable chemical. The chemical solution thus prepared reacts with the metal surface and produces an adherent coating of the metal compound. The following two types of the chemical coatings are important:

1. **Chromatic Coatings.** In this process, the metal to be coated is dipped in the solution of sodium dichromate and concentrated nitric acid. The chromatic coated surface provides adequate resistance to corrosion. It is generally provided for protection of zinc, aluminium, magnesium parts etc.
2. **Phosphate Coatings.** In this process, the metal to be coated is dipped in a hot solution of manganese dihydrogen phosphate at 90°C for about 45 minutes. The phosphate coated surface provides adequate resistance to corrosion. It is generally provided for the protection of iron, steel, zinc, aluminium; tin parts etc.

   The phosphate coating has an excellent property *i.e.*, it has the ability to retain paint and provide lubrication when necessary. It is usually done before painting the surface to give an organic finish and to provide corrosion resistance to the surfaces of refrigerators, washing machines, automobile parts, outdoor electrical fittings etc.

3.19 VITREOUS ENAMEL COATINGS

The vitreous enamels are glass-like materials having wide range of composition. The constituents of enamel may be borax, alumina, iron oxide, cobalt oxide, soda titanium, salt petre, quartz, tin oxide, felspar, fluospar, magnesia and other substances which are required to give colour or other physical properties. All these constituents are smelted together at 1200°C and are grounded in the form of powder with water to form a fine slurry. The slurry is then applied on cleaned objects by dipping or spraying. It is then dried and heated in a furnace to a temperature around 850°C.

The vitreous enamel coatings have good corrosion and chemical (except alkalis and hydrofluroic acid) resistance. They may be applied to both ferrous and non-ferrous surfaces.

3.20 CERAMIC COATINGS

The ceramic coating is similar in character to vitreous enamels, but it has high refractoriness. In this process, the coating material (high refractory, oxides such as aluminium oxide, chromium oxide, cobalt oxide or beryllium oxide) is applied to the metal by dipping or spraying.

The ceramic coating protects the metal against oxidation and corrosion at high temperatures. It is used in the making of nozzles, vanes and blades of gas turbines, air-crafts, rocket propulsion systems, thermo-couple tubes, cutting tools etc.

REVIEW QUESTIONS

1. What do you understand by corrosion? Name the different methods used to prevent it.
2. Discuss the various methods used for cleaning of metals.
3. What method is used for
   (*a*) removing oil and grease from the metal surfaces, and
   (*b*) removing oxides, dirt and scale from the metal surfaces.
4. Explain the following metallic coatings:
   (*a*) Galvanizing (*b*) Electroplating, and
   (*c*) Anodizing.
5. What are the main ingredients of an oil paint? Explain their functions.
6. Write short notes on :
   (*a*) Varnishes; (*b*) Lacquers, and
   (*c*) Enamels.
7. Why plastic and chemical coatings are applied on metals?
8. What is the difference between vitreous enamel coating and ceramic coating?
9. Describe metal spraying-wire and powder processes and their applications.

OBJECTIVE TYPE QUESTIONS

1. The process of providing a thin layer of zinc coating on iron and steel is called
   (*a*) electroplating (*b*) galvanising
   (*c*) metal cladding (*d*) cementation
2. The process of providing a thin layer of phosphate on steel is called
   (*a*) perkerizing (*b*) terne coating
   (*c*) calorising (*d*) Anodizing
3. In order to clean the surface of robust parts, the method preferred is
   (*a*) tumbling (*b*) abrasive blasting
   (*c*) chemical cleaning (*d*) none of these
4. In electroplating
   (*a*) the base metal acts as cathode and the coating metal as anode
   (*b*) the cathode and anode are dipped in a solution containing some salt of the coating material, *i.e.*, electrolyte
   (*c*) a direct current is passed through the electrolyte
   (*d*) all of the above
5. Which of the following statement is correct?
   (*a*) The process of providing a thin layer of tin on iron or steel sheets is known as electroplating.
   (*b*) Galvanised utensils are used for preparing food.
   (*c*) The process of providing a comparatively thicker layer of coating on metal surface is called metal cladding.
   (*d*) all of the above
   (*e*) none of the above
6. Calorizing is a process of providing thin layer of
   (*a*) aluminium (*b*) chromium
   (*c*) zinc (*d*) both (*a*) and (*b*)
   (*e*) both (*b*) and (*c*)
7. In an oil paint, turpentine oil is used as a
   (*a*) base (*b*) vehicle
   (*c*) pigment (*d*) solvent
8. The constituent which provides a body to an oil paint is called
   (*a*) base (*b*) vehicle
   (*c*) pigment (*d*) solvent

9. The solution made by dissolving nitrocellulose, resin and plasticizer in a solvent, is called
   (*a*) paint (*b*) enamel
   (*c*) lacquer (*d*) varnish
10. Which of the following protective coating is applied to protect the metal against oxidation and corrosion at high temperatures?
   (*a*) paint (*b*) ceramic coating
   (*c*) vitreous enamel coating (*d*) enamel

ANSWERS

1. (*b*)	2. (*a*)	3. (*a*)	4.(*d*)
5. (*c*)	6. (*a*)	7. (*d*)	8.(*a*)
9. (*c*)	10. (*b*)		

Chapter 4

Gear Manufacturing and Fininshing Processes

4.1 INTRODUCTION

Gears are used for transmission of power and used widely in automobiles, agricultural machinery, industrial machinery, machine tools, oil engine etc. With rapid industrialization the gears are called upon to yeild noise free operation, ensure high load carying capacity at a constant velocity ratio. The wear and fatigue strength of the gear tooth is the factor that governs its durability and reliability and depends to a certain extent on the manufacturing technology employed.

4.2 CLASSIFICATION OF GEAR PRODUCTION METHODS

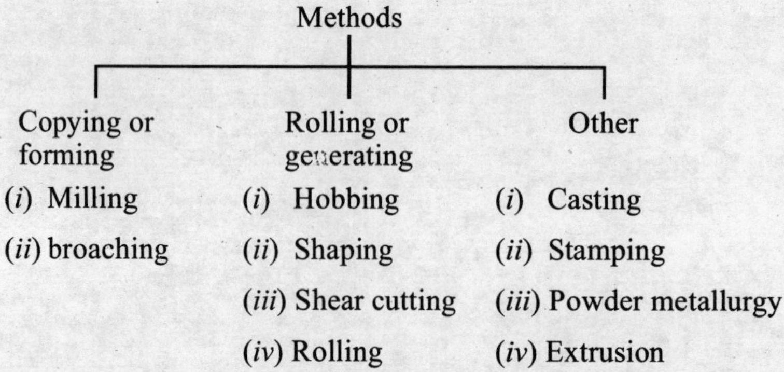

The methods mentioned above yield varying degree of accuracy and hence limited field of application. We shall discuss some of the important gear forming and generating methods.

4.3 MILLING

Milling machines are capable of cutting practically, every type of gear by employing an universal indexing mechanism and a form cutter. The cutter has the required tooth profile on it.

This cutter may be operated on a vertical type or horizontal type of milling machine. In both cases the cutter rotates on the spindle and work reciprocates under the cutter. Once the cutter finishes a tooth profile the work is indexed for the next position.

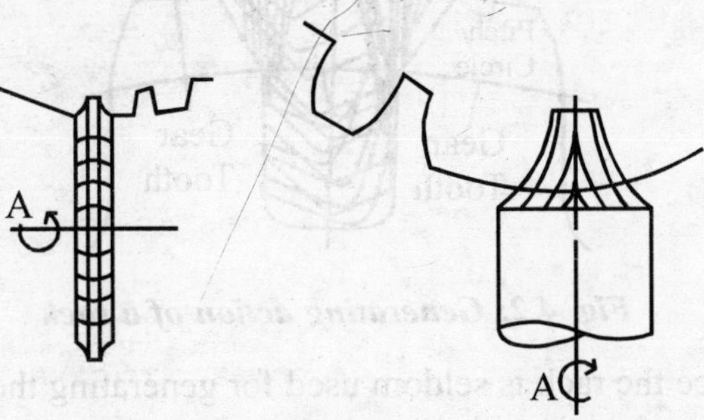

Fig. 4.1

It is important to keep In mind that two successive teeth should never be milled one after the other because the heat due to metal cutting may distort the teeth. It would be very much safer to finish the teeth on the gear blank after short intervals.

Cutting gears on a milling machine is a very common practice because one cutter with a fixed module number is used for cutting teeth on a blank, irrespective of its diameter, as long as the pitch and module remain same. The practice does not fall in line with the gear theory, according to 'gear theory' different gears with different number of teeth but same module differ to some extent in tooth profile. If the theory is to be rigidly followed then a set of cutters should be employed. A most common type of set possesses eight cutters, but sets with 15 cutters are also available.

4.4 THE PROCESS OF GEAR GENERATING

The term generating in gear cutting stands for development, of involute curve by straight cutting edges of the cutter, which produces, a series of facets of the blank so as to form the involute profile. The cutter and the blank, behave as two mating gears in working contact. This generating action is easier to follow with reference to a rack and a pinion. Let the rack be made out of a hard metal and pinion blank from a softer-material say, plastics, (Fig. 4.2) on moving the rack over, the, plastic blank and permitting the blank to rotate about its own axis the rack will copy the profile of its teeth on the blank. The linear speed of both, being kept same. In actual practice since the blank is of metal therefore, copying is not possible and as such the rack teeth should perform cutting action. This cutting action is obtained by reciprocating the rack cutter about an axis which is perpendicular to the paper or parallel to the axis of the blank. After each cutting stroke the blank is rolled through one pitch while the cutter conducts return stroke. The reciprocating speed of the cutter is quite high. The generating action of the rack is diagrammatically represented in Fig. 4.2 which shows the successive position of the gear relative to rack developing involute profile.

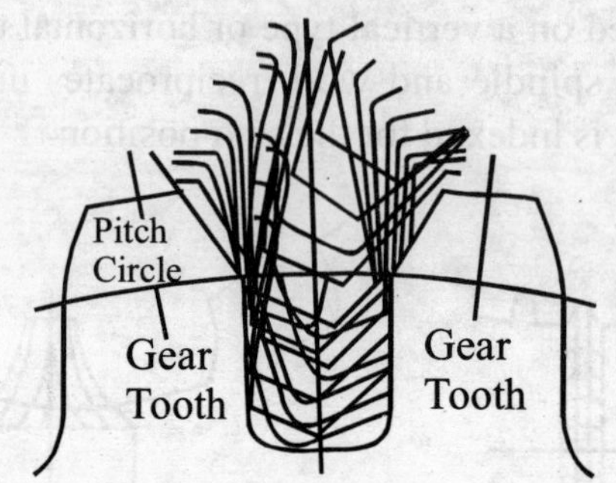

Fig. 4.2: Generating action of a rack

In gear cutting practice the rack is seldom used for generating the teeth. The cutter is either a pinion or a worm with relieved cutting edges.

4.5 GEAR HOBBING

Hobbing is a process of generating a gear by means of a cutter, called a hob, that revolves and cuts like a milling cutter. A hob may be briefly described as a fluted steel worm, equipped with proper clearance for rotting action. Flutes are cut across the threads, forming rack-shaped cutting teeth. The threads may be right or left-hand, and the flutes may be straight or helical. A hob may have one, two or more threads, 'Single thread (or start) hobs are generally used, although where a high degree of accuracy is desired on gears of coarse pitch, a roughing cut is taken with double or triple-thread hobs and the finishing cut with a single-thread hob. A single-thread hob cuts but one tooth, whereas double thread hob cuts two teeth concurrently.

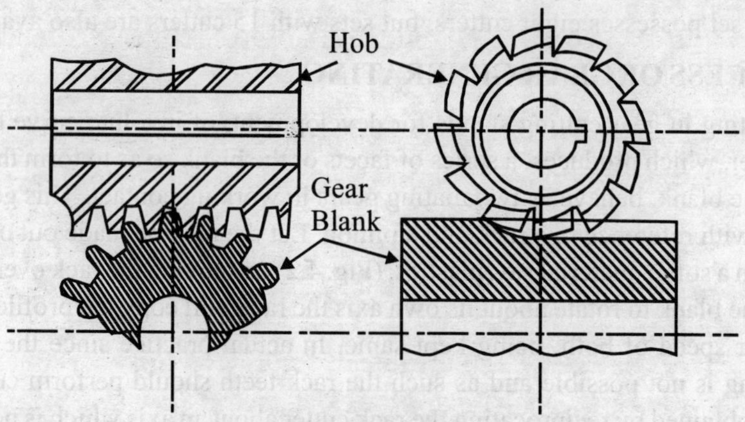

Fig. 4.3: Gear hobbing

In gear hobbing, the gear blank is first moved in towards the rotating hob until the proper depth is reached. The action is the same as if the gears were meshing with a rack. As soon as the proper depth is reached the hob cutter is fed across the face of the gear until the teeth are complete, both gear and cutter rotating during the entire process. Gear hobbing is shown in Fig. 4.3.

In hobbing spur gears, the hob is set with its teeth parallel to the axis of the gear blank, and the hob and gear blank rotate in a relationship that indexes the gear blank in time with the advancing lead of the thread on the hob. At the same time, the hob is fed slowly across the face of the gear blank to finish the teeth. In hobbing helical gears, the axis of the hob is set over an angle to produce the proper helix, and rotation of the gear blank and hob relative to each other must be accelerated or retarded to produce helical teeth. Worm gears may be cut with the axis of the hob set at right angles to the gear and the hob is fed tangentially as the gear rotates.

Hobs are made to any desired gear tooth form or pitch but will generate only that form or pitch. Any number of teeth may be hobbed with a given hob the number of teeth being determined by the ratio of the revolutions of the hob to the revolutions of the gear blank.

The hob axis is set at an angle, equal to helix angle of the thread in reference to the axis of the gear blank. This brings the blank teeth in the plane of the hob's teeth. This plane is termed as generating plane. The cutter finishes all the teeth in it's one pass over the work. For cutting helical gears the hob must be set over an additional amount equal to the helix angle of the gear.

To start the cutting, the hob is located so as to clear the-blank and then moved inward until proper setting for tooth depth is obtained. The hob is then fed towards the gear blank in a direction parallel with the axis of rotation of the blank. As the gear blank rotates, the teeth are generated and the feed of the hob across the face of the blank extends the teeth of the desired tooth face width.

Although the hobbing process is often associated only with the manufacture of gears and splines, many other forms may be cut. Its also an economical method of producing ratchets, sprokets and other special forrns.

The versatility of hobbing makes it an economical method of cutting gears, one hob of a given module will cut the teeth of all involute spur and helical gears of the same normal pitch and pressure angle including all number of teeth and helix angles. The size of teeth and the size of workpiece are limited only by the capacity of the hobbing machine. Hobbing is applicable to all types of gears of ferrous, non ferrous and non-metallic materials. Carbide tipped hobs can be used for mass production.

4.5.1 Hobbing Machines

Hobbing is done on single-purpose hobbing machines. So far as design is concerned, there are two basic types: horizontal work spindles, and vertical work spindles. At present, the vertical type is more widely used. Multiple spindle machines are used when the production requirement are high.

The hob spindle has two adjustments. First the tool head is mounted on a swivel base so that, the axis of the hob spindle may be set at an angle to the axis of the work spindle. The angle depends on the helix angle of the hob and the kind of gear being cut. And second, the hob spindle may be adjusted axially as a means of distributing wear on the tools.

A high rate of production is secured on hobbing machines because the cutting action is continuous in one direction. Gear hobbers generally produce spur and helical gears as well as splines and chain sprockets. They cannot produce unsymmetrical shapes, and because of the rotary cutter, the hobber cannot cut as close to a shoulder as a machine using a reciprocating tool.

4.5.2 Hobbing Machines: Hobbing Machine Relationship

The generating process requires an accurate relationship between various elements of the machine, in order to produce the desired result. For a spur gear with a single thread hob the blank rotates one tooth-space while the hob rotates once. The rotation is timed by means of change gears. For helical gears the rotation of the work is slightly advanced or retarded in relation to the hob rotation and the feed also bears a definite relationship with the work and hob.

The following relationship are typical for some makes of hobbing machines. To maintain the required relationship between the index and feed, there are two constants which are established by the gearing in the machine and are used to determine correct change gears. The "Machine-index constant" it is the number of revolutions of the hob spindle during one revolution of the work spindle when the index change gear have a ratio 1 : 1.

The "Machine-Feed Constant" is the distance in mm which the hob slide will advance during one revolution of the work spindle when the ratio of the feed change gears is 1 : 1. These constants are normally shown on the machine.

For the machining of spur gears, the index ratio (IGR) can be determined by:

$$\text{IGR} = \frac{n \times \eta}{N}$$

n = Number of threads on hob

η = Machine index constant.

N = Number of teeth In the gear and feed gear

ratio = F/M

F = Feed in mm per revolution of the work

M = Machine feed constant.

If helical gears are to be cut, the Index gear ratio (IGR) is calculated as

$$\text{IGR} = \frac{\eta \times C \times n}{CN \pm 1}$$

Where C is a constant.

The selection of positive or negative sign in the above relationship is determined by the hand of the hob, the hand of the gear and the direction of feed.

The constant C in the above equation is obtained from the relationship.

$$C = P_n / F\psi$$

Where P_n = Normal circular pitch

ψ = helix angle.

For spur gears, the head swivel angle is equal to the head angle of the hob. The practice for determining the swivel angle for helical gears is to add the lead angle of the hob to the helix angle of the gear if they are of opposite hands and to subtract if they are of same hand.

4.5.3 Hob Speed and Feed

Hob speed is primarily a function of machinability of the material being cut, the hob specification, the machine capacity and the hob life desired. The hob tooth form and material should also be taken into account.

The amount of feed varies with the finish and accuracy required the machine capacity and the tooling. A high feed rate produces long, deep feed marks resulting into rough surface. Table 4.1 gives the speed and values commonly employed for hobbing.

TABLE 4.1

Recommended speed and feed for the hobbing of spur gears

Material	hardness BHN	module	feed mm/work rev.	hob speed m/min	HSS tool material
Free Machining	100–150	5–25	1.125	70	S_4
Carbon Steel Low C. Steel	100–150	5–25	1.125	80	S_4, S_2
Med. C. Leaded	125–175	5–25	1.125	70	S_4, S_2
Med. C. Steel	125–175	5–25	1.13	57	S_4, S_2
High C. Steel	175–225	5–25	1. 27	48	S_4, S_2
Grey C. Iron	125–150	5–25	0.95	60	S_4, S_2
Wrought Al alloys	30–80	5–25	0.95	300	S_1, S_2
Wrought Cu-alloys	10RB–70RB	5–25	0.95	210	S_4, S_2

4.5.4 Estimating Hobbing Time

Hobbing length (L) would comprise of approach, face width and over run. The hobbing time can be computed from the relationship as,

$$\text{Hobbing time} = \frac{NL}{n \times rpm \times F}$$

Where, rpm = hob rotational speed

The approach is the distance from the point of the initial contact between the hob and blank to the point where the hob first cuts at full depth. This distance varies with the hob diameter, depth of cut and the hob swivel angle.

The over-run can be calculated as equal to :

$$\text{over - run} = b\cos\psi \frac{\tan S}{\tan \phi_n}$$

where, ϕ_n = Pressure angle

ψ = Helix angle

S = Swivel angle

Ex. 4.1: A single start hob has 60 mm pitch diameter and right hand helix is to be used to be for making standard spur gear of cast iron. If

Number of teeth	=	30
Module	=	3 mm
Pressure angle	=	20° at full depth
face width	=	30 mm
diameter of hob	=	50 mm
Feed of hob per revolution of blank	=	2 mm

Determine rpm of the gear, angle between hob axis and work axis, radial depth of cutter and cutting time.

Sol.: (*i*) rpm. of the gear

Assuming a cutting speed of 15 m/min the hob rotates at

$$= \frac{15 \times 1000}{\pi \times 50}$$

$$= 96 \text{ r.p.m.}$$

For 30 teeth to be cut, the hob must rotate by 30 revolutions therefore, when hob is set for 96 rpm the blank should rotate at for every 3.2 rpm w/p revolutions.

(*ii*) As the teeth are arranged along the hob axis, its axis is to be tilted with respect to the work axis for cutting straight spur gears. This inclination is equal to helix angle. It is obtained by

$$\tan w = \frac{\text{Lead}}{\text{n} \times \text{hob pitch dia}}$$

$$\text{Pitch of the hob} = \pi \times \text{module} = 3 \times 3.14$$

$$= 9.43 \text{ mm}$$

$$\text{Lead of the hob} = 9.42 \times 1 = 9.42 \text{ mm}$$

$$\tan \text{w} = \frac{9.42}{\text{n} \times 50} = 0.060$$

$$\text{w} = 3.4°$$

hence the required angle = 90° – 3.4° = 86.6° **Ans.**

(*iii*) Radial depth of cut

$$= 2 \text{ addendum} + \text{clearance}$$

$$= 2 \text{ module} + 0.25 \text{ module}$$

$$= 2 \times 3 + 0.25 \times 3$$

$= 6.75$ **Ans.**

$$(iv) \text{ Cutting revolution} = \frac{30+6}{2} = 18\left(6\,mm = over\ run + approach\right)$$

$$\text{Cutting time} = 18/3.2 = 5.66 \text{ min.}$$

Ex. 4.2: A single threaded hob is to be used for cutting a 80 teeth gear. If the hob diameter is 40 mm, hob travel is 60 mm and it is rotating at 100 rpm. find the cutting time. Also determine the reduction time if triple threaded hob is used. The feed may be assumed as 4 mm.

Sol.: The feed is expressed as movement of hob per revolution of gear blank, therefore during a traval of 60 mm the gear shall make $\left(\frac{60}{4}\right)$ revolutions or 15 revolutions.

while teeth are being shaped.

$$\text{Hob revolutions} = 15 \times 80$$

$$= 1200$$

$$\text{Actual cutting time} = \frac{1200}{100}$$

$= 12$ min for single thread when triple start hob is used the gear moves through 3 revolutions during the time hob executes 80 revolutions.

No of hob revolution/gear revolution.

$$= \frac{80}{3}$$

Hob revolution for 15 gear blank

$$= \frac{80}{3} \times 15$$

$$\text{Cutting time} = \frac{1200}{3 \times 100}$$

$= 4$ min. **Ans.**

External types of gears can be easily cut by hobbing. Not only spur and helical gears are possible to cut by this method but even worm and worm wheels splines and sprockets can also be given pitch out involute type spur and helical gears of the same pitch and pressure angle, irrespetive of the number of teeth on the blank and the helix angle. Further, the process is quite capable of producing those profiles which are symmetrical (involute) and non-symmetrical (ratchet teeth).

4.5.5 Factors Effecting Accuracy of Hobbed Gears

The factors that govern the accuracy of hobbed gears are:

(*i*) Accuracy of the hobbing machine
(*ii*) Quality of the hob and hob mounting
(*iii*) Accuracy of work holding fixture
(*iv*) Miscellaneous factors such as machinability of the work material speed feed etc.

The machine tool characteristics that affect the work accuracy are:

(*i*) True running of hob arbor end work spindle,
(*ii*) parallelity of the hob movement with respect to work spindle,

Axial slip of hob and work spindle,

Indexing error in the gear train,

Hob head vibration,

Errors in axial feed screw,

Thermal effects, and

Rigidity of the machine structure.

The quality of hob used in a particular case also determines the accuracy of the gear produced. In this regard the grade of hob selected should be consistent with the accuracy requirement of the finished gear like roughing, semifinishing and finishing. The gear accuracy is also influenced by the errors introduced during hob resharpening. The-principal element affected by the hob resharpening are:

(*i*) Position of the cutting face

(*ii*) Pitch of the flutes,

(*iii*) Direction of the flutes, and

(*iv*) Finish of the cutting face.

4.5.6 Advantages of the Hobbing

(*i*) Due to the absence of indexing, reduction in cutter approach and continuous cutting action the production rate is high.

(*ii*) Heat generated due to metal cutting is uniformly distributed over the entire work and therefore, the possibility of distortion in the gear is minimum.

(*iii*) High degree of accuracy can be maintained on the products over large period.

(*iv*) Control over tooth spacing, lead and tooth profile is easier.

(*v*) All types of spur and helical gears can be cut on metals and non-metals.

(*vi*) A large number of similar gears held on a mandrel can be cut at a time. This reduces the approach time of the hob.

4.5.7 Limitations

(*i*) Internal gears can not be cut by this method.

(*ii*) Gears which have shoulders and flanges cannot be cut by hobbing.

4.6 GEAR SHAPING

At the beginning of this century another method of gear cutting was introduced to industry by E.R. Fellows which today is a versatile method of manufacturing the gears. Credit is given to Fellows Gear Shaper Co. for many facet developments carried out in this field with the method both internal and external gears can be manufactured.

Gear shaping method is based on generation action which is achieved due to the movement of two meshing gears. One of them. *i.e,*. pinion, is a cutter while the other is a blank. The cutter makes several facets during its cutting action as the cutter and work rotate. This type of cutting action of the cutter is also known as *moulding generating action*. The cutter is mounted on a vertical ram in a slide reciprocating just as in a shaper through a crank arm mechanism. At the same time the cutter also rotates about its vertical axis. The work, however, has the rotary motion, Fig. 4.4.

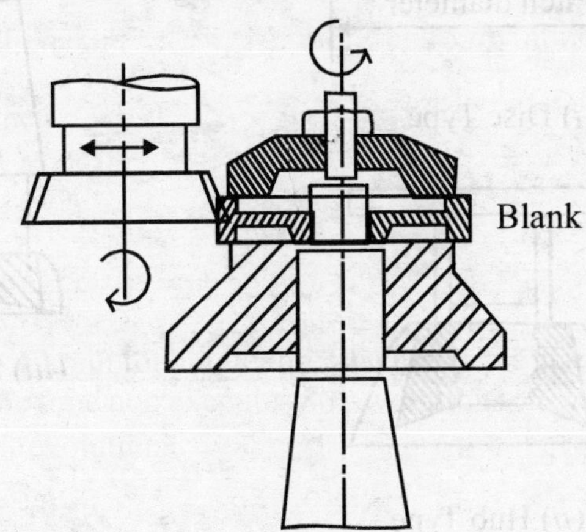

Fig. 4.4: Set up on a gear shaper

While operating the machine tool, the pinion like cutter is moved aside and the work is loaded on the work arbor. The machine is next started and the cutter is radially feed into the work for the required depth. The feed is given to the cutter while the work is revolving. In the end cutter is made to go through the gear at least once after the desired depth has been attained on the blank. To avoid the cutter rubbing over the cut surface during its return stroke, the work is mounted on a relieving mechanism.

The basic nature of the cutter is that of a spur gear each tooth of which has been relieved and shaped for forming proper cutting edge. These cutters are of three types:

(*i*) Disc type, (*ii*) Shank type and

(*iii*) Hub type Fig. 4.5 for proper cutting.

4.6.1 Advantages

(*i*) One cutter of a right tooth size, pitch and pressure angle can cut gears of various sizes from the smallest pinion to the largest gear which can be easily held on the machine.

(*ii*) Certain non-conventional types of gears *i.e.,* eliptical gears, face gears, cluster gears, gears with flanges and shoulders etc. can only be cut by gear shaping method.

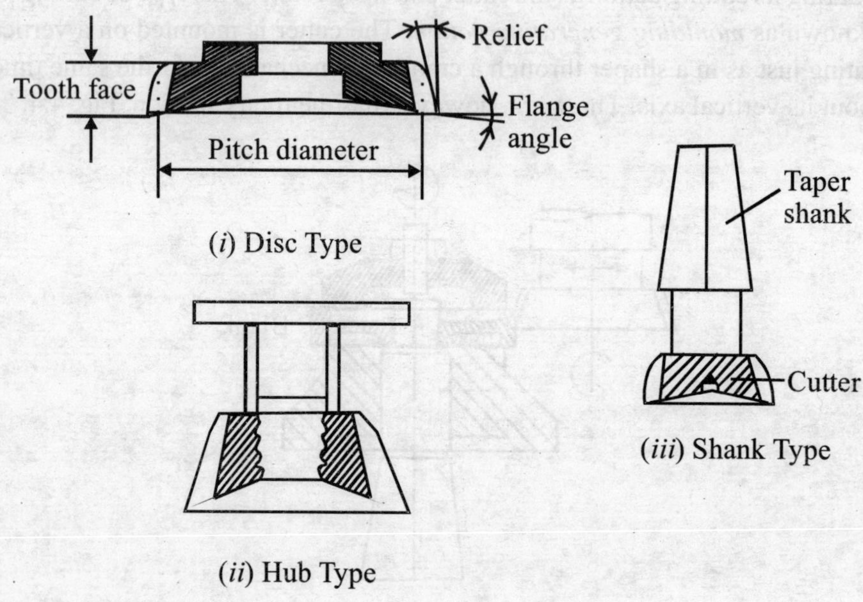

Fig. 4.5: Types of shaper cutters

(*iii*) It offers a very high degree of accuracy as the chips of uniform are cut by the cutter.

4.6.2 Limitations

(*i*) The length of cut is shorter therefore, gears with wider flanks cannot be produced.

(*ii*) The production rate with a gear shaper is lower than hobbing because of differing nature of the motion of the cutter.

(*iii*) For cutting helical gears with different helix angles different helical guides are needed.

(*iv*) Only one gear can be cut at a time.

A considerable interest has been shown by certain automobile industries in U. S. A. to make transmission gears by rolling methods instead of shaping hobbing and Ford motor Co. has claimed much closer tolerances and greater accuracy of the gears made out of rolling in their pilot line. Such a process gives more reliablity, longer tool life, less floor space, more uniform production, greater consistency and higher strength due to grain flow orientation.

4.7 HOBBING V/S MILLING

1. In millinig the gear teeth can be cut with the use of a milling cutter that has been formed to the shape of the tooth to be cut. As each tooth is cut, the gear blank is rotated to new position and then the succeeding cut is made. Thus, it is not suitable for mass production.

   This method sometimes produces distortions due to errors in the indexing or concentration of heat of cutting which is concentrated at one place

2. The hobbing method produces gears by means of a hardened cutter called a hob. The production of gears is accomplished having the hob rotate in fixed relationship to the gear blank. With this action, there is provided a rolling action of the gear in relation to the hob.
3. The important difference between hobbing and milling is that a generating action takes place in the production of hobbed gears whereas a milled tooth gear has a contour predetermined by the shape of cutter alone. The true involute profile produced during hobbing because the process provides a true rolling action that further gives maximum smoothness in operation and longest cutter life. Hobbing also, provides a uniform velocity. Milling however does notproduce exact involute profile. When considerable variety of gears are to be produced in small quantities and large diameter gears are to be made milling is preferred over hobbing.

4.8 HOBBING V/S SHAPING

1. Due to continuous process of cutting and indexing and non-reciprocating motion of the hob, the hobbing process is faster as well as more accurate. The heat liberated during cutting is uniformly distributed on the cutter and the work, therefore, the distortion of gears tooth is never a problem with hobbing. Hobbing machines are much simpler and more rigid in construction because of a few motions involved during cutting. Hobs are easier to manufacture from accuracy point of view.
2. Shaping enjoys wide popularity for one simple reason that it can cut internal types of gears at very fast rate. Due to shorter stroke of the cutter, it is possible to cut those gears which have flanges and shoulders in close proximity. Some non-conventional type of gears can only be cut by this process. A large number of identicial and accurate teeth are difficult to make on shaper cutter.

4.9 BEVEL GEAR CUTTING

Straight bevel gears are cut on a spacial purpose gear cutting machine tool which employs two 'half tooth' tools. One of it cuts one face of the tooth while the other one cuts the other face of the same tool. Both of these tools are mounted on a cradle and have reciprocating motions, in opposite directions. At the start, the cradle carrying the tools is rolled in upward position and the blank and cradle are set for required tooth depth. The machine is next started when the tools start reciprocation and the cradle gradually rolls down moving the blank also along with it. This movement accomplishes the generating action. By the time cradle reaches the extreme downword position the tools completes the tooth profile. The cradle is than rolled back and the tools perform the finishing operation on the tooth profile. When the cradle reaches the starting position, the blank is withdrawn and indexed for next tooth.

Small and straight tooth bevel gears are cut with the help of two disc type cutters. The cutters roll with the blank and produce the teeth.

Bevel gears with curved tooth profile are made on another type of generating machine by employing a circular rack type face mill cutter. The cutter axis is parallel to the axis of the roll of the cradle. For cutting, the blank is fed inside towards the cutter to the full depth. The cradle is in its downmost position. Both of them roll together in upward direction. The cutter engages the blank from the small end and moves towards the large end or across the width of the tooth face.

4.9.1 Bevel Gear Generating Process

The fundamentals of bevel gear generating process involves the rolling of a bevel gear blank on a crown wheel. The crown wheel is a bevel gear having pitch cone angle of 180°. The, teeth of the crown wheel are straight and radial and are provided on the flat face of the gear. In the bevel gear generating process, the crown wheel may be considered as a rack cutter. In practice, however, only one tooth on the crown wheel acts as a cutting tool and the relative movement between the tool and the work is such that it resembles the rolling action of the blank on the crown wheel.

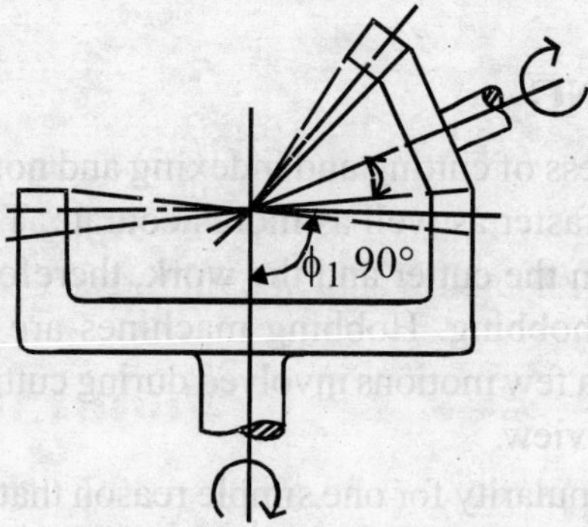

Fig. 4.5 (A): A bevel gear in mesh with a crown gear

4.10 WORM GEARS

Use of worm and worm wheel enables us to obtain a large driver to driven gear ratio. For example, to achieve a gear ratio 1 of 40 : 1 the worm wheel should have 40 teeth for a single start worm wheel only 20 teeth for a 2-start worm. The worm and worm wheel axes are normally at right angles, this would mean that the helix angle of the worm wheel must match the worm helix.

4.11 GEAR SHAVING

It is a process of finishing gear teeth by running the gear at high speed in mesh with a *gear shaving tool* which is in the form of a *rack* or *pinion*. The teeth of the shaving tool are hardened, accurately ground and their faces are provided with *serrations*, as shown in Fig. 4.6. These serrations form the cutting edges which actually provide a sort of scraping operation on the mating faces of the gear teeth to be finished. The gear is pressed into contact with the shaving tool and the latter rotated at high speed. The gear also rotates in mesh with the tool and is also reciprocated simultaneously. The shaving tool carries a little inclined teeth so that their axes can be crossed as the two come in contact. This prevents the jamming of the two. The above relative motion of the gear and the shaving tool results in a highly finished surface on the gear teeth. When a rack type tool is used, the gear is mounted on a reciprocating arbor and is brought in mesh with a horizontal rack situated under it. The rack is reciprocated longitudinally at high speed and the gear across it. The lengthwise movement of the rack type tool also rotates the gear. Shaving with rack-type tool, however, suits only small gears. The shaving tools, although costly, have a fairly long life.

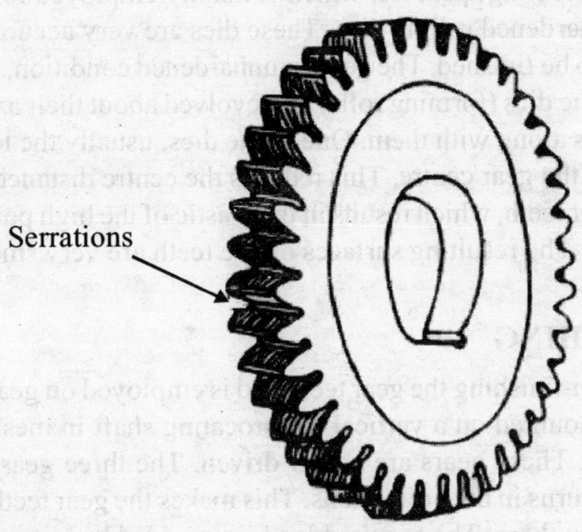

Fig. 4.6: A gear shaving tool

4.12 ROLL FINISHING

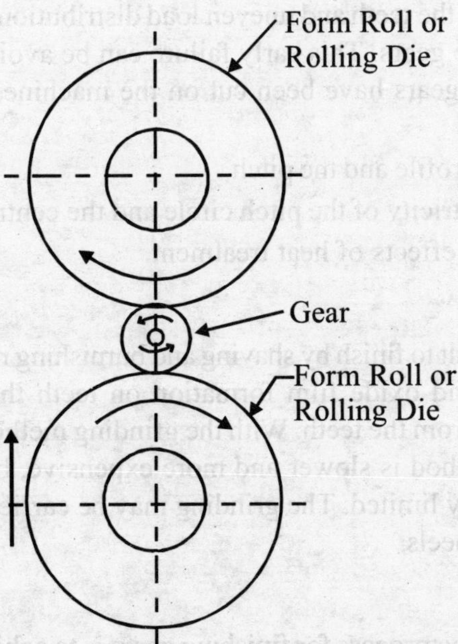

Fig. 4.7: Roll finishing a gear.

It is a *cold rolling* (forming) process, which is mainly employed for finishing helical gears. It involves the use of two hardened rolling dies. These dies are very accurately formed to contain the tooth profile of the gear to be finished. The gear, in unhardened condition, is set between the two dies, as shown in Fig. 4.7. As the dies (forming rolls) are revolved about their axes, the gear, being in mesh with the rolls, also rotates along with them. One of the dies, usually the lower one, while rotating is also fed radially towards the gear centre. This reduces the centre distance between the two dies and exerts pressure on the gear teeth, which results in the plastic of the high points and burrs deformation, if any, on the tooth faces. The resulting surfaces on the teeth are very smooth and the tooth profiles highly accurate.

4.13 GEAR BURNISHING

It is also a cold process for finishing the gear teeth and is employed on gears after cutting but prior to hardening. The gear is mounted on a vertical reciprocating shaft in mesh with three hardened and ground burnishing gears. These gears are power driven. The three gears are fed into the cut gear and rotate through a few turns in both directions. This makes the gear teeth surfaces smooth and also imparts a little hardness to them. The required load is provided by pneumatic, hydraulic or electric means.

4.14 GEAR FINISHING METHODS

None of the methods for manufacturing of gears on machines can produce gears of very accurate dimensions and shape. Any error in the gears due to these reasons may lead to noisy performance of the gear box. Irregular wear of the teeth and uneven load distribution on the teeth. They are sufficient to cause an early failure of the gears. This early failure can be avoided by subjecting the gears to a finishing operation, after the gears have been cut on the machines. This finishing operation may specifically be used for:

(*i*) Rectifying the tooth profile and the pitch,

(*ii*) Maintaing the concentricity of the pitch circle and the central hole, and

(*iii*) Elemination the after effects of heat treatment.

4.15 GEAR GRINDING

Hardened gears are very difficult to finish by shaving and burnishing methods. Since the heat treatment may cause sever distortion and oxide film formation on teeth therefore, there is a necessity of removing considerable stock from the teeth. With the grinding method it is possible to finish the heat treated gears. Though the method is slower and more expensive, but it guarantees highest quality gears. Therefore, its use is very limited. The grinding may be carried out on generating principle or employing formed grinding wheels.

4.16 GEAR LAPPING

The object of employing lapping process for finishing gears is to achieve a very high degree of finish. Gears are subjected to lapping after they have been finished by burnishing. Lapping is carried out with the help of two or three cast iron gears which carry abrasives. The C. I. gears are made to run in contact with the gears and a flow of very fine abrasive is maintained over the contact zone when the lapping takes place in the usual manner. As lapping can remove very small amount of metal, this process of finish only correct small errors maximum upto .05mm only.

4.17 GEAR HONING

Honing is the last operation performed on hardened gears. It also helps in correcting gear errors. Honing removes minor nicks and burrs, gives a fine surface finish on the gears contacting surfaces. Gears so finished find applications in gear trains where a low noise level is desirable.

4.18 GEAR BURNISHING

It is not a common method of gear finishing. In this method the gear is rolled under pressure with three hardened, accurately formed burnishing gears. It is cold working process in which any high points on the tooth surface are plastically deformed to get accurate and finished tooth profile. However, the operation may have a smeared metal surface.

REVIEW QUESTIONS

1. On what basis do you classify the gear cutting methods?
2. Describe the principle of gear generating.
3. Sketch a hob, show its various elements on it.
4. How is a gear made by the process of shaping.
5. Distinguish between hobbing, shaping and milling.
6. What are various methods of finishing the gears?
7. How does gear-lapping differ from gear-honing?
8. What kinds of gears are made by broahing process?
9. How is hobbing time defined?
10. Calculate time taken to hob a spur gear having 72 teeth with a single threaded hob running at 75 rpm and having a feed of 2.5 mm per blank revolution. The width of face of gear is 35 mm. **(Ans. 9.6 min)**

Chapter 5

Finishing Processes

5.1 INTRODUCTION

Surface finish is considered an important property of any industrial product as it describes its surface texture. A study of surface finish enables to determine the deviations from the nominal surface described by an engineering drawing. Different machining operations generate different characteristics. Surfaces generated by turning, milling, shaping, planing, grinding and superfinishing show marked variations when compared with each other. The variation is judged by the degree of smoothness. A surface generated by super-finishing is the smoothest one while, that by planing is the roughest surface. This kind of Judgement is based on visual inspection and it fails to differentiate between surfaces produced by same machining operation but under different cutting conditions. A basis of quantitative evaluation is required in place of qualitative assessment. While defining the assembly and the fit of two mating parts it becomes absolutely necessary to describe the surface finish in quantitive terms which is a measure of micro irregularities on the surface and expressed in microns. Also for proper function, low bearing friction, wear rate or to prevent stress concentrations, it may be necessary to avoid or to have certain roughness profiles.

Machined surfaces are produced by a combination of two motions — (*i*) relative longitudinal motion of the tool or job and (*ii*) transverse movement of the tool or job. The previous is due to inherent action of the production process and the later is due to feed marks. The deviation from the established criteria when extends over the whole surface appears, Fig. 5.1, in the form of:

(i) Lack of flatness,

(ii) Out of roundness, and

(iii) Taper forms into barrel form

Two types of deviation are noted:

(i) Macro-geometrical deviation (L_1/H_1) large, and,

(ii) Macro-geometrical deviation (l_3/h_3) small.

5.1.1 Macro-geometrical Deviations

These are single deviations from the ideal geometrical form and extend over the whole surface being tested. Out of roundness, lack of flatness, taper forms to barrel form are examples of such deviations. They are created due to in accuracies of slides and wear of guides over long use. These are ctiaracterised by the large ratio of length L_1 of the surface to its deviation h_1, from the proper form, Fig. 5.1. Ratio $\frac{L_1}{H_1}$ should not normally be greater than 1000. However, if this value is required to be less for proper functional requirement of the deviation should be specified in drawing.

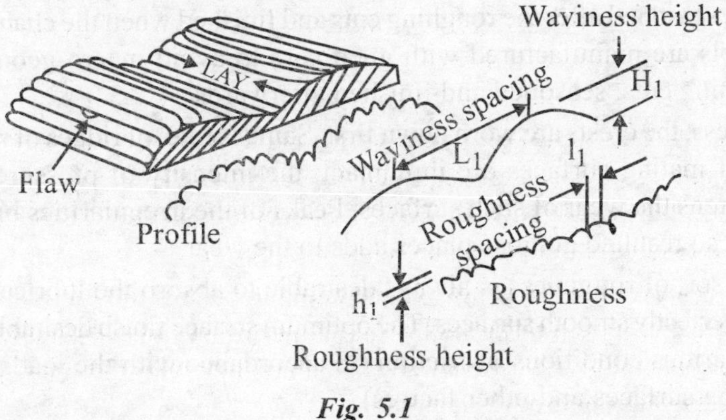

Fig. 5.1

5.1.2 Micro-geometrical Deviation (Surface Roughness)

These are also a series of regularly repeated deviations of a wave, with a ratio of pitch to height L_3/h_3 comparatively quite small and approximately equal to 50. These deviations are produced by the trace of an edged cutting tool and plastic flow of the metal during machining. Usually, these are finer irreguilarities in the surface texture and is termed as surface roughness. To describe the surface roughness, the height of the irregularities is measured and rated in microns and its width in mm.

Flaws: Irregularities that occur at one place or at relatively frequent intervals on the surface such as a ridge, hole, peak, crest or valley are called flaws. Unless or otherwise specified the flaws shall not be included in the roughness measurement.

Waviness: Waviness is the usually, widely spaced component of surface texture and it is normally of wider spacing than the roughness width of cut off. Waviness may result due to such factors as machine or work deflections, vibrations, chatter, heat treatment or warping strains.

Waviness Height: It is rated in mm as the peak to valley distance.

Waviness Width: Waviness width is rated in mm as the spacing of successive wave peaks or successive wave valleys.

The measurement of waviness is quite different from the average roughness, since maximum peak to valley and wavelength dimensions are specified. Waviness is usually measured with dimensional gauges referenced to a master surface such as an optical flat.

Lay: Lay is the predominant direction of the surface pattern. This is normally determined from the method a job is produced.

5.1.3 Effect of Surface Quality on Functional Properties

The quality of the surface finish of running and sliding parts has a great deal to do with how long these items would last. It has a marked influence on the following functional properties of machined parts.

1. Wear Resistance: Larger macro-geometrical deviations cause non uniform wear at different sections of a surface. Projecting areas of the surface are worn off first. Macro-geometrical deviation may occur where roughing cuts are applied to castings, due to unbalancing of inner stresses. Therefore, such castings, may be seasoned after the roughing cuts and finished when the changes have stabilized. Beds of machine tools are manufactured with great care to avoid macro-geometrical deviations. They are given roughing cuts, seasoned and finished afterwards.

In case of waviness, the crests are worn down first. Same is true, of ridges of micro-irregularities. As only the crests of mating surfaces are in contact, the intensity of pressure over these places become high and hastens the wear of such surfaces. Peaks of the irregularities break the lubricating film, and dry friction so resulted at those places adds to the wear.

However, some sort of roughness is always desirable to absorb the lubricating oil film which cannot be retained in perfectly smooth surfaces. The optimum surface finish desirable can be established experimentally, for various conditions of friction (in accordance with the load, speed, lubrication, material of the bearing surfaces and other factors).

2. Fatigue Strength: The valleys between ridges of a machined surface may become the focus for the concentration of internal stresses. These valleys between ridges behave like notches and a crack may start from these notches which are points of high stress concentration. Many such cracks lead to subsequent destruction of the machine part and is said to have failed by fatigue caused by stress concentrations.

3. Strength of Interference Fits: When a part is press-fit into another, the actual interference obtained in press fitting a part with a rough surface would differ from that obtained from a smooth part (having the same measured diameter of the press fitted surface).

4. Corrosion Resistance: The resistance of machined surface against corrosive action of liquids and gases, water, air, acids in lubricant etc. is greatly influenced by the quality of the finish. The deep valleys of a rough surface have a capacity to contain more corrosive substances which cause corrosion in the depth of metal. A highly finished surface has few valleys, and the corrosion in depth of metal will be less.

5.1.4 Factors Affecting Surface Finish

Quality of machined surface depends on many factors which can be listed as below:

(*i*) The material of workplace,

(*ii*) Type of machining operation,

(*iii*) Rigidity of machine-work-tool system,

(iv) Type, form, material and sharpness of cutting tool,

(v) Cutting conditions, and

(iv) Type of cutting fluid used.

5.1.5 Numerical Evaluation of Surface Finish

Many methods have been developed to express the surface finish, numerically. These numerical values are obtained with respect to a datum. Two such datums have been described a little afterwards. Some of the well-known methods for reading the values of surface profiles are given below:

1. Peak to valley Height Method.
2. Centre Line Average Method.
3. Root mean Square Method.

5.2 REPRESENTATION OF SURFACE ROUGHNESS

The surface roughness is represented in Fig. 5.2. If the machining method is milling, sampling length is 2.5 mm, direction of lay is perpendicular to the surface, machining allowance is 2 mm and the representation will be as shown in Fig. 5.2 (b).

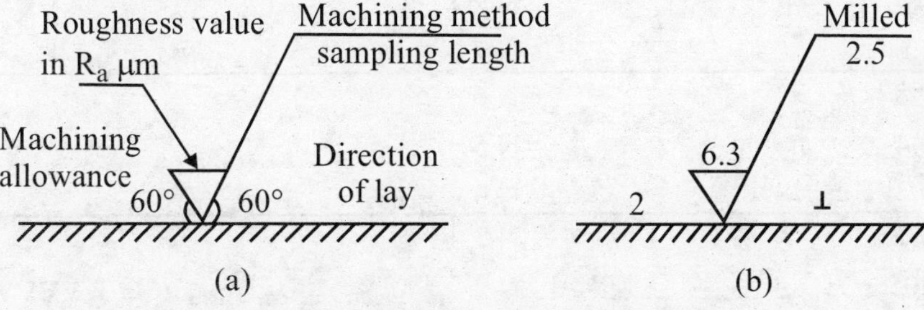

Fig. 5.2: Representation of Surface Roughness

(*i*) The limits of surface roughness can be represented as:

$R_{a16.0}^{8.0}$ or $R_a^{8.0-16.0}$

(*ii*) The surface roughness and sampling length can be represented as:

R_a 8.0 (2.5)

Here surface sampling length is 2.5. mm.

(*iii*) The surface roughness and Lay can be stated as:

R_a 1.6 Lay Circular

However, in most cases, one single piece of information is sufficient which is indicated as follows:

The I.S.O. has recommended a series of preferred roughness values and corresponding roughness grade numbers to be used when specifying surface roughness on drawings. These values and grade numbers are listed in Table 5.1.

The roughness symbols indicate the practice followed in the industry.

Another method adopted is: N8 ∇/ and so on.

Table 5.1 Roughness Value

Roughness Values $R_a\,(\mu m)$	Roughness grade number	Roughness Symbol
50	N 12	~
25	N 11	∇
12.5	N 10	
6.3	N 9	
3.2	N 8	∇∇
1.6	N 7	
0.8	N 6	
0.4	N 5	∇∇∇
0.2	N 4	
0.1	N 3	
0.05	N 2	∇∇∇∇
0.025	N 1	

5.3 SURFACE FINISHING PROCESSES

In a manufacturing plant, a product may be shaped, turned, milled or drilled, and left in that condition as being satisfactory for use. However, if a better finish is desired, for looks, for accuracy, for wearing qualities, or for any other reasons, one of the microfinishes that include lapping, honing, super-finishing, polishing, buffing, may be employed. In soine cases other operations are done only to get durable finishes.

5.3.1 Lapping Process

It is an abrading process employed for improving the surface finish by reducing roughness, waviness and other irregularities on the surface. It is used on both heat-treated and non-heat-treated metal parts. It should, however, be noted that where good appearance of the job surface is the only requirement, it should not be employed; since there are other finishing methods which will give the same desired result with low cost. It should be used only where accuracy is a vital consideration in addition to the surface finish. The basic purpose of lapping is to minimise the extremely minute irregularities left on the job surface after some machining operation.

In brief, we can say that **Lapping** is basically employed for removing minor surface imperfections, obtaining geometrically true surfaces and better dimensional accuracy and, thus, facilitate a very close fit between two contacting surfaces.

Material: The material to be selected for making a lapping tool of lap largely depends upon the individual choice and the availability, and no specific role can be laid for the same. The only consideration that has to be made is that the material used for making a lap should be soft so that the abrasive grains can be easily embedded in its surface. In case a hard material is used for making the lap, the abrasive particles will quickly go out of their places. The commonly used materials are soft cast iron, copper, brass, lead and sometimes hard wood.

Abrasives: All the abrasives, *i.e.*, natural as well as artificial are used for lapping. Aluminium oxide is preferred for lapping soft ferrous and non-ferrous metals. Silicon-carbide and natural corundum are used for hardened steel parts. Powdered garnet is used for lapping soft ferrous and non-ferrous metals; emery for hardened steel components and diamond for extremely hard materials like cemented carbides.

Vehicle: The term 'Vehicle' in lapping denotes the lubricant used to hold or retain the abrasive grains during the operation. To some extent it also controls the cutting action of the latter. Some common vehicles used in laping include the vegetable or olive oil, lard oil, water soluble oil, mineral oil, kerosine mixed with a little machine oil, alcohol, and heavy grease. For cleaning the laps, naptha is commonly used. No specific recommendations can, although, be laid for the selection of a particular vehicle, still the vehicle used should possess the following qualities.

1. It should be able to hold the abrasive particles uniformly during the operation.
2. Its viscosity should not be considerably effected by temperature changes.
3. It should not evaporate quickly.
4. It should be non-corrosive.
5. Its viscosity should suit the operating speeds.

Lapping Allowance: The lapping operation is not primarily meant for removing metal. As such, enough care should be taken to ensure that too much material is not left on the work surface to be removed by lapping. The endeavour should always be to obtain as good surface finish through earlier machining operations as it is possible so that a very negligible amount of stock remains to be removed by lapping. It should be borne in mind that smaller the amount of stock left, quicker will be the lapping process and higher will be the dimensional accuracy obtained. Keeping in view the above discussions, the recommended range of lapping allowance to be left is as follows:

1. *General lapping work.*

Allowance on surface	0.0075. mm to 0.0125 mm
Allowance on dia or thickness	0.015 mm to 0.05 mm

2. *For lapping to work which has been finish ground.*

Allowance on surface	005 mm
Allowance on dia.	0.01 mm.

Pressure and Speed for Lapping

The following magnitudes of pressures are recommended for lapping:

For soft materials 0.07–0.2 bar

For hard materials 0.07bar

Normal *speed range* used in *rotary lapping, i.e.*, when the work and lap have a rotary motion relative to each other, varies from 1.5 m/sec to 4.0 m/sec.

5.3.2 Types of Lapping Operation

Lapping operations can be broadly classified into the following two main groups.

1. Equalising Lapping 2. Form Lapping

1. Equalsing Lapping: It is the operation of running two mating parts or shapes together with an abrasive between them. When two such surfaces run together in constant contact with the abrasive, their surface finish is improved and any deviation of shape is corrected. Those results can be easily seen during seating of tapered valves in their seats or when gears are rotated together with these objectives.

2. Form Lapping: As is clear from the name itself that it is not merely rubbing of surfaces together but it is the *shape* of the lap that is responsible for finishing a corresponding work surface. Obviously, the *lap* used in the operation will be a *form lap, i.e.*, containing the shape to be lapped.

5.3.3 Lapping Methods and Machines

Lapping is done in the following two ways:

1. By hand ------------ called *hond lapping*..
2. By machines ------------ called *machine lapping*.

5.3.4 Hand Lapping

In hand lapping, either the lap or the work-piece is held by band and the motion of the other enables the rubbing of the two surfaces in contact. This method is widely used in lapping press work dies, moulding dies and metal moulds for casting, limit gauges, etc. In some cases the lapping compound is placed between the two surfaces and the two are robbed together by moving one of these by hand, the other remaining stationary. A few examples of this method are lapping of surface plates, engine valve and valve seat, etc. Whatever may be the method used, out of the above two, it is necessary that the work and lap are not rigidly guided with regard to one another and that their relative movement is kept along an ever changing path, *i.e.*, not repeated along the same path. For example, Fig 5.3 shows the bottom surface of a hardened steel piece being lapped on a *cast iron plate*. The top surface of the *plate* is made perfectly plane, finely finished and checkered by providing cross grooves, as shown. These grooves help in collecting excess abrasive grains and removed chips.

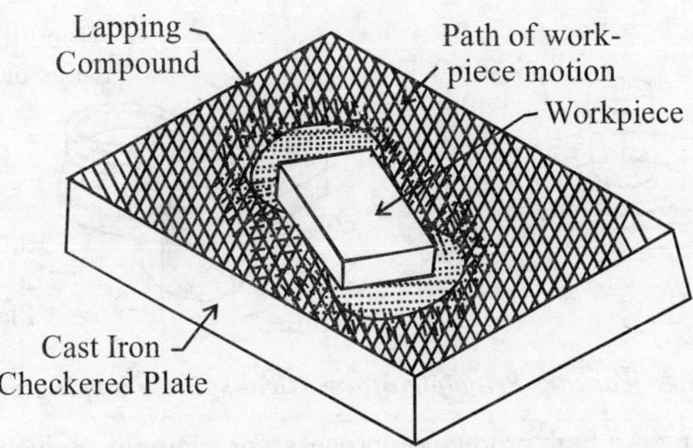

Fig. 5.3: An example of Hand Lapping

Before commencing the operation, the *lapping compound (fine grained abrasive)* is spread over the top surface of the plate. *Grey cast iron* which is porous and soft, is the material used for the plate. It is, therefore, able to retain the *abrasive grains (lapping medium)*. The workplace is placed over the lapping medium and rubbed over the same. As already indicated above, the movement of the workpiece has to be along an irregular path, not just to and fro. In this case, the workpiece is shown moving along a path taking a shape of English numeral '8'.

5.3.5 Machine Lapping

Machine lapping is performed for obtaining a highly finished surface on many articles like races of ball and roller bearings, gears, crankshafts, machine bearings, pistons, pins and gauges, gauge blocks, various automobile engine parts and micrometer spindles, etc. Many different types of machines are used in lapping. A typical vertical spindle machine consists of *two wheels* (circular plates), one above and the other below. The workpieces are placed between the two and the loose abrasive grains with vehicle are fed. A modification of this machine consists of two bonded abrasive wheels in place of the above rotating wheels. Obviously, no loose abrasive is required in this case. In both the machines, the lower wheel rotates and the upper one does not, but floats over the workpieces. These two machines can be used only for circular and flat work.

The working principle of a typical *Vertical Spindle Lapping Machine* is shown in Fig. 5.4. The workpieces are loaded in *conditioning rings* or *cages* on the *rotary lower plate* which rotates about a vertical axis, as shown. At the same time, the conditioning rings also rotate along with the workpieces in their own positions. The combination of these two rotary motions provides a gyratory motion to the workpieces, due to which the entire surfaces of the two plates are covered. This results in an even wear of the plate surface and, therefore, its flatness is maintained. The upper plate just provides a floating action and helps in maintaining parallelism. Most of the commonly used engineering materials can be lapped by this type of arrangement. In case of slender jobs, a workholder is incorporated between the two lap plates to keep the workpieces in alignment with the plates.

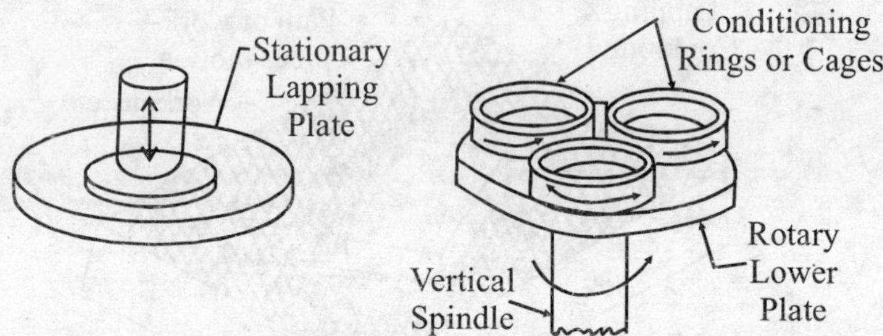

Fig. 5.4: Working Principle of a vertical spindle lapping machine

Mechanical lapping is a high production process, for example, gudgeon pins 25 mm diameter and 75 mm long are lapped at the rate of 500 pieces per hour, removing 0.05 to 0.075 mm of material with a limit of accuracy of roundness, straightness and size within 0.025 mm. Mechanical lapping machines are of vertical construction with the work holder mounted on the lower table which is given an oscillating motion. The upper lap is stationary and floating, while the lower one revolves at about 60 rev/min. Several types of lapping machines are available for lapping round surfaces. A special type of centreless lapping machine is made for lapping small parts such as piston pins, ball bearing races etc.

The following are examples of work done by lapping: aircraft piston pins, automotive wrist pins, diesel engine injector-pump parts and spray nozzles, plug gauges, certain dies and moulds, gauge blocks, reftigerator-compressor parts, oil-burner parts, micro-meter spindles, roller bearings, taper rollers, worm and worm gears, crankshafts, camshafts, ball bearing raceways etc.

During machine lapping, a pressure of 0.007 to 0.02 N/mm^2 for soft materials and upto 0.07 N/mm^2 for hard materials is satisfactory. Mechanical lapping machines can be used for lapping: (*i*) External cylindrical surfaces, and (*ii*) flat surfaces.

A general purpose machine for lapping both cylindrical and flat surfaces is shown in Fig. 5.5. A number of workpieces are placed between the upper and the lower lap, whose surfaces have previously been lapped flat. The workpieces are placed in slots in a workholder so that their axes x-x are not quite radial. The shape of the slots will depend upon that of the workpieces. The two laps are rotated and the workholder is given as oscillation of about 25 mm amplitude. A stream of vehicle in which fine abrasive flour is suspended is fed to the centre of the laps and flows outwards and the workpieces are thus gradually lapped to size.

Lapping has become a common production process with the demand for hardened surfaces having only a few micrometers of surface finish. However, because, it is such a slow method of metal removal, it is obviously relatively expensive and is not economically justified unless operating requirements make such surface finishes absolutely necessary.

Lapping and polishing differ in the following manner—Polishing is meant to produce a shiny surface whereas a lapped surface does not usually have a bright shiny appearance. Lapping definitely removes metal from lapped surface, whereas, polishing as a rule does not remove any appreciable amount of metal. Lapping improves the geometrical shape of the body, whereas, polishing does not. Lapping is essentially a cutting process, while polishing consists of producing a kind of plastic flow of the surface crystals so that the high spots are made to fill the low spots.

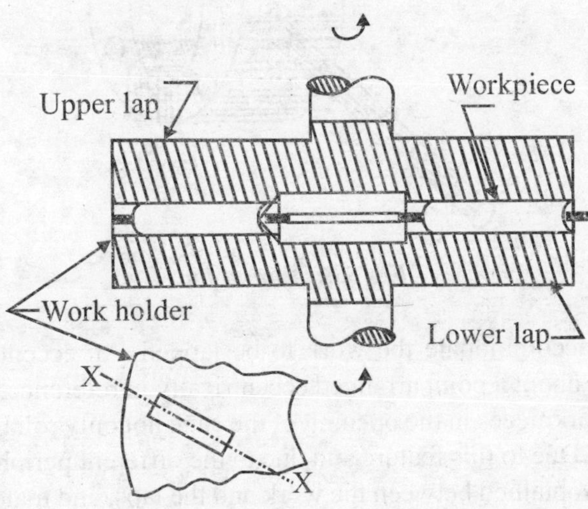

Fig. 5.5: Machine Lapping

Some modem lapping machines are provided with vibratory motion instead of rotary motion, the lower plate carrying an abrasive paper fixed on its top surface. Workpieces are held over this paper by providing light pressure from the top plate. The lower table is vibrated and, as a result, the workpieces flow on the emery paper for lapping.

For lapping crank-shafts and pins, etc. an abrasive-belt machine is commonly employed. This machine is a horizontal spindle machine, of which the spindle carries the crankshaft. During the operation, the crankshaft gets a small reciprocating motion. This machine neither uses the embedded abrasive laps nor the bonded wheels. Instead of them, coated abrasives like paper or cloth are used.

A centreless grinding machine can be conveniently adopted to perform lapping operation for round objects. The bonded wheels used in this case will be sufficiently large so that the workpiece is subjected to the abrasive action of the wheel for a longer period on each pass. Another special feature of these wheels will be that they will have their grains of a much finer grit. Rest of the setting and operation will be quite similar to entreless grinding. External surfaces of revolution can be lapped either on ordinary lathes with hand laps, (Fig. 5.6) or on special lapping machines.

Such a special lapping machine has cast iron discs, (mounted on vertical spindles. The lower lap is rigidly secured to its spindle while the upper lap is swivel-mounted so as to align with the lower lap surfaces.

The upper and lower spindles rotate at different speeds. A movable cage is arranged between the laps.

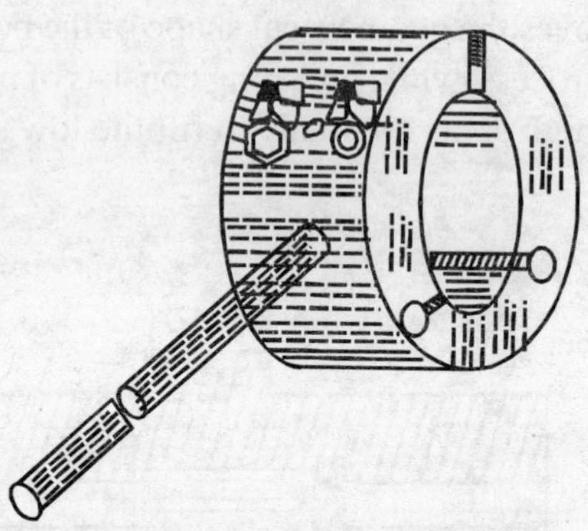

Fig 5.6: A hand lap

It has openings to accommodate the work to be lapped. An eccentic mechanism imparts a rotary motion to the cage about a point arranged eccentrically in reference to the centre of the lower lap. Consequently, the workpieces in the opening of the cage not only roll between the laps but have an axial movement, also. Due to this feature and due to the different peripheral speeds of the laps, a relative sliding motion is obtained between the work and the laps, and material is removed from the work surface.

Lapping of Holes: Laps for holes consists of sectors ranging from 2 to 6 number mounted on the arbour and expanded by springs or cones, Fig. 5.7.

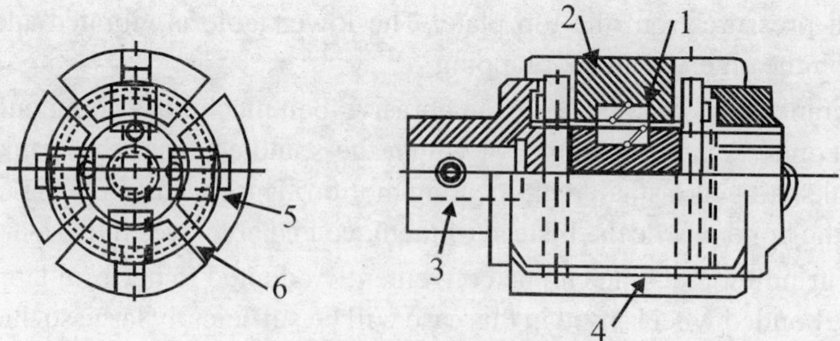

Fig. 5.7: A lap for holes.

The lap is inserted into the hole wherein, it is rotated and reciprocated. Surfaces of laps are charged with a lapping compound. Holes are rarely lapped in production shops due to slow production however, lapping is used for finishing holes in tool room ring gauges.

Bonded Abrasive Lapping: Lapping compounds tend to leave a dark, dull surface that is hard to remove. Solid bonded, abrasives are used on machines to remove the lapping compound and improve the finish.

5.4 HONING PROCESS

If lapping action resembles to that of grinding, the honing operation resembles to turning. The only point of difference is in number of cutting edges operating on the work surface in the case of honing. The honing operation is more productive than lapping for finishing of holes. Instead of a lap and lapping compound, it uses fine abrasive grits held within the binding material of the honing material of the honing stone. The development of honing stone is now-so advanced that it is possible to hone all metals including non-ferrous metals, aluminium alloys etc.

Honing is carried out at low speeds. The honing stone has a tendency to build up material removed during the process which tends to increase the local heat. The lubricant and coolant used during the lubrication does not flush out the microchips and therefore cooling and chip removal is not very efficient. Thus, nigher speeds will cause excessive heat generation. Usually, the honing operation is done at 10–30 m/min. This cutting velocity is a resultant of the stroke velocity and the peripheral velocity of the stone. This process maintains the surface finish between 0.2 μm to 0.05 μm and tolerances within $\pm$ 0.002 mm. The ten most common errors in bore production like bow, taper, out of round, waviness, diameter bell mouth and barrel, boring tool marks, misalignment and reamer chatter are removed by honing. Out of roundness and taper may also be eliminated.

***(i)* Honing Process:** The workpiece must be rigidly clamped on to the work-table. Care must be taken to keep the bore exactly parallel to the axis of the hone spindle. The bore must be centred on the spindle not with the honing awl, which is coupled via a ball joint but instead directly with the spindle itself, to an accuracy of 0.1–0.2 mm. It is necessary to set up the job exactly, inspite of the flexible joint, if precise bores are required. The form of the bore can be damaged with the slightest sideways pressing of the honing awl.

The stroke and working length must finally be adjusted, which the hone must follow in order to obtaing a good cylidrical bore.

A good practical rule is for the honing stone to over run the bore by 1/8 of its length above and below. Care should however, be taken that the stone is not longer than 60% of the depth of the hone stone that are too long usually given increased diameter at the start and end of the bore, as the ginding surface of the stone decreases when it over runs at the end of the bore due to a part of leaving contact. Because of the constant advance pressure on the awl, the specific pressure increases correspondingly at the ends and this leads to a longer rate of metal removal.

When honing is done manually, the tool is rotated, and the workpiece is passed back and forth over the tool. For precision honing, the work is usually held in a fixture and the honing tool is given a slow reciprocating motion as it rotates. Honing stones may be loosely held in holders, cemented into metal shells which are clamped into holders, cemented directly in holders or cast into plastic tabs which are held in holders. Some stones are spaced at regular intervals around the holder, while others are interlocking so that they present a continuous surface to the bore. A typical honing tool head is shown in Fig. 5.8. The honing tool may be so made that a floating action between the work and tool prevails and any pressure exerted in the tool may be transmitted equally to all sides. Coolants are essential to the operation of this process to flush away small chips and to keep temperatures uniform.

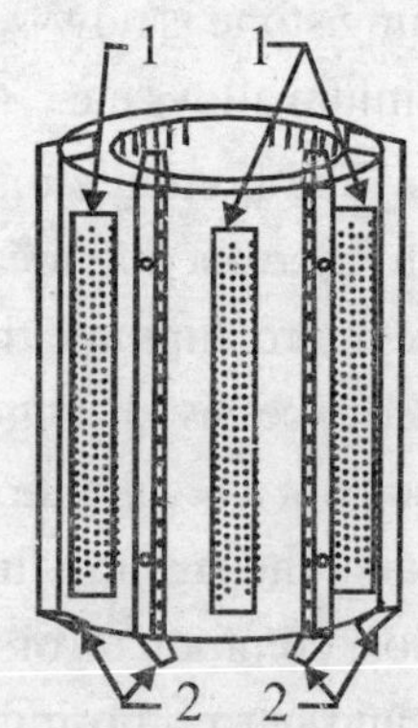

Fig. 5.8: Honing tool-hed for holes 1. Stones, 2. Guides

Most honing is done on internal surfaces, or holes, such as automobile cylinders. There are a few applications of honing to external surfaces. Parts can be of any shape, but the surface must be cylindrical. Practically any material can be honed. Soft materials which cannot be lapped, can be honed because of the use of bonded abrasive. Hard and soft cast iron, steel, carbides, bronze, aluminium, brass and silver, as well as glass, ceramics and some plastics can be honed.

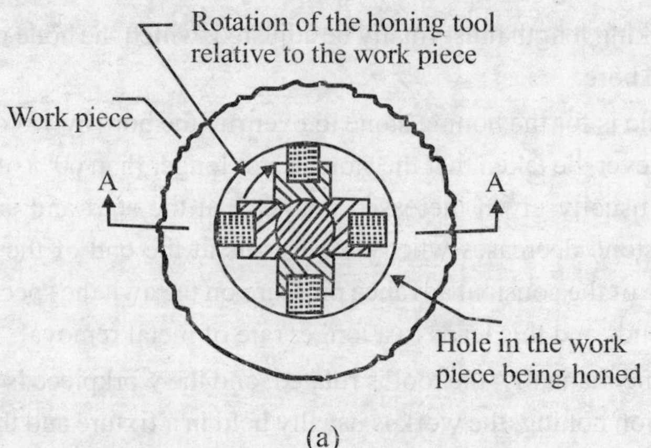

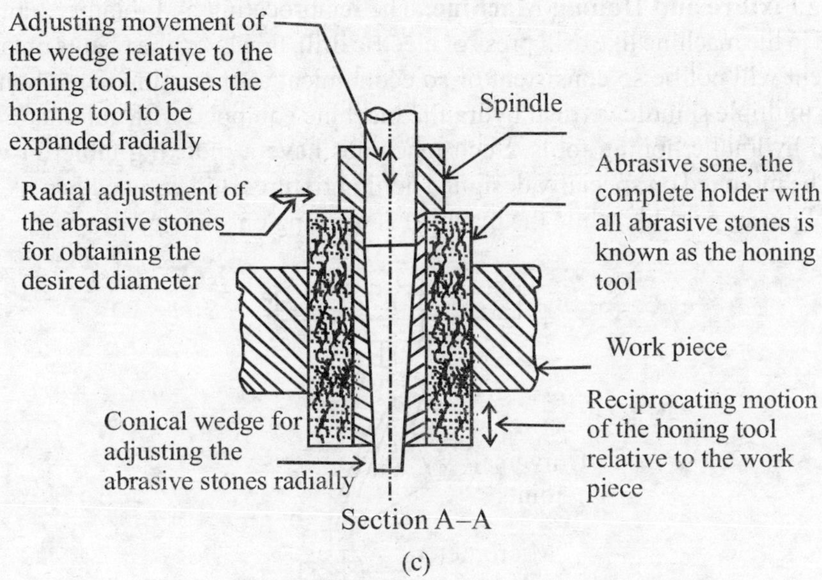

(c)

Fig. 5.9: Honing Tools

Honing machines are similar in general construction to vertical drilling machines, but the spindle reciprocation is usually by hydraulic means. The rotary motion may be from a hydraulic motor or by gearing. The speed ratio of two motions affects the work finish and may be varied throughout the operation or for different materials. For cast iron, the speed ranges from 1.0 to 2.5 m/s for rotation; with 0.25 to 0.35 m/s for reciprocation. The corresponding speeds for steel are 0.75 to 1.0 m/s for rotation and 0.2 m/s for reciprocation. The reciprocation motion distributes the wear over the whole length of the sticks and keeps the bore cylindrical. Semiautomatic honing machines used in the finishing of automobile cylinder bores are of vertical type. Both single and multispindle machines are used for this operation. The abrasive stones are mounted on a honing tool. In order to expand the abrasive stones outward to fit the hole to be honed, the conical wedge is moved relative to the honing tool, Fig. 5.9.

Honing of external surfaces can be successfully accomplished by mounting 4 sticks held in holders on contracing yoke The Workpiece is rotated while the sticks envelope the workpiece. Only hand pressure is applied on the sticks.

The spindle speed in honing is larger than number of strokes. The honing allowance on steel parts is about 0.05mm, A hone 20 mm and, 65 mm long can remove 0.00375 mm per minute in hardend tool steel and 0.10 mm mintue in annealed steel SAF 1000. Abrasive sticks for honing are made of grit (aluminium oxide, silicon carbide or diamond) bond (vitrified caly or resinoid) and air voids. The way in which these factors are balanced determines how the abrasive will act on any particular part. Abrasive sticks with grain size of 30 to 500 are used for honing.

***(ii)* Honing Fixture and Honing Machine:** The reciprocating and rotatory motion of a hone can be produced in the machine like drill press or electric drill, however, the results obtained with this type of equipment will not be so consistent or so economical as those done on a honing machine, which may be a multiple spindle vertical hydraulic machine equipped with automatic bore gauging size control and hydraulic honing tools. Such machines have a indexing table on which several workpieces can be mounted on specially designed honing fixtures. Indexing table makes the loading and unloading of pieces possible while the machine is working on some piece.

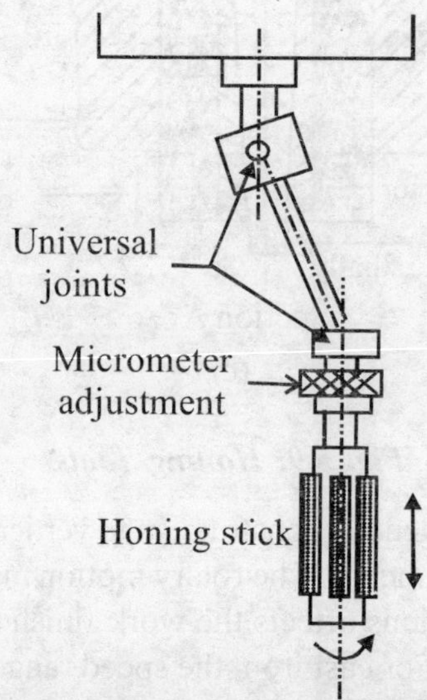

Fig. 5.10: Vertical Honing Machine

A general arrangement of a vertical honing machine is shown in Fig. 5.10. The abrasive sticks (upto 8 in number) are expanded while -honing takes place, if required, by micrometer controlled, mechanical or hydraulic, means. The honing tool will follow the axis of the original hole, therefore, the honing tool or fixture must be free to float. This is done by using universal joints as shown in the figure. Due to this, the honing tool becomes self center and it is not necessary to line up the hole and hone axes precisely. Vertical machines have been designed for work upto 500 mm diameter.

Horizontal honing machines are used only for honing large, long gun barrels and similar work. The workpiece is held on the left and the tool is rotated and reciprocated by the head on the right end of the bed of the machine. Machines of this type are made with strokes of upto 22.5 m and hone holes as large as about 1m in diameter.

All honing gives a smooth finish with a characteristic cross hatch appearance. The depth of these hone marks can be controlled by variations in pressure, speed and type of abrasive use. Accurate dimensions can be maintained by the use of automatic size controlled devices in connection with honing. Typical applications of honing are finishing of automobile engine cylinders, bearings, gun barrels, ring gauges, piston pins, shafts and flange faces.

The grit size of abrasive material used in abrasive sticks is 80 to 180 for primary honing and 300 to 500 for secondary honing. Surface finish of the order of 0.05 μm R_a can be obtained by honing.

(*iii*) Advantages of Honing:

1. Several holes may be honed simultaneously, on multiple spindle machines.
2. Holes of any diameter or length may be honed.
3. A high degree of accuracy and surface finish can be obtined.
4. Relatively high productivity as compared to lapping:

(*iv*) Disadvantages

Tough non-ferrous metals cause glazing or clogging of the voids of the abrasive sticks and thus, they are difficult to hone.

A new development in the field of honing is development of diamond honing wheel for cast iron. It is now extensively used on soft and hard steels, cemented carbides, aluminium and brass. Part like cylinder blocks and liners, refrigerator compressors, gears and connecting rods are processed by diamond honing.

5.5 SUPER FINISHING PROCESS

Previously ground external surfaces of steel, cast iron and non-ferrous alloys are finished by abrasive sticks as in honing to a very fine accuracy by the method called super-finishing. The abrasive stone or the stick is mounted on the end of a pring loaded quill. The assembly has an oscillating mechanism by which the stone can move back and forth parallel to workpiece axis a maximum distance of 5 mm

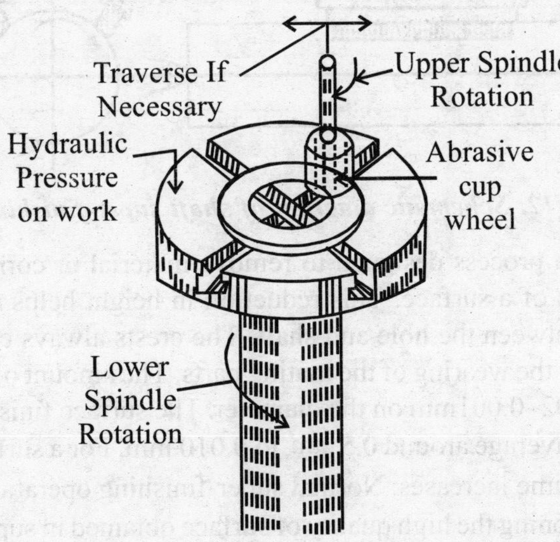

Fig. 5.11: Super Finishing of flat surfaces

at 424 cyles/min. The assembly can be mounted on the cross slide of a lathe or on machine especially designed for the purpose. The traversing motion to the stick is also provided, if the job is larger than length of sticks. The stone is formed to the radius of the work by putting emery cloth over the workpiece face. As the stone contacts the emery cloth it is soon worn to the radius of the Job, it is brought in contact with the work at about or kgf /cm2 pressure. The part is rotated at a speed equal to 20 mm. The oscillator motion is started and coolant (a mixture of kerosine and oil) is used to flood the area. If the job is long the traverse motion is also given along with oscillatory motion to the abrasive sticks.

It is employed to practically, get rid of the peaks and valley within a sub-microsopic range.

Flat surfaces can also be super-finished according to this principle in which there should be two spindles, Fig. 5.11. The lower spindle holds the work and rotates it. The upper spindle is a spring loaded quill on which a stone is mounted. The upper spindle only rotates at off centre position. It need not oscillate however it can traverse if the work dimensions demand it. Super-finishing process utilises an abrasive stock of very fine grain size (400 to 600). Longitudinal feed or traverse of the stick is 0.1, 0.15 mm per revolution of work finished by this method.

A special lubricant, usually a mixture of kerosene and oil, is used to obtain a high quality of surface finish. A schematic diagram of shaft super-finishing is shown in Fig. 5.12.

Special general-purpose machine tools are available for super-finishing. Other types of ordinary machines, in particular, lathes, are sometimes employed for this purpose. Single purpose machine tools for example, for finishing crankshaft jorunals, camshafts, etc. are also used.

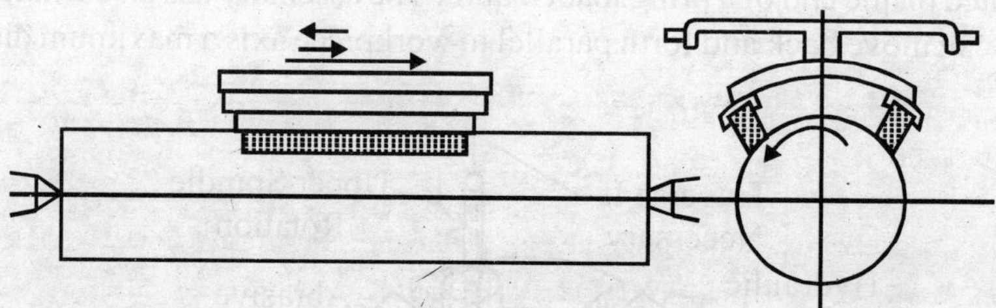

Fig. 5.12: Schematic diagram of shaft super-finishing

Super-finishing is not a process designed to remove material or correct part geometry as in honing. It reduces the crests of a surface. This reduction in height helps in the maintenance of a proper film of lubrication between the hole and shaft. The crests always create the danger of film being punctured and quicken the wearing of the mating parts. The amount of material removed from the part may range from 0.002–0.001mm on the diameter. The surface finish produced ranges from less than 1 to 0.80 μm with average around 0.5 μm to 0.010 mm. For a surface to be smoother than 0.5 μm the super-finishing time increases. Normal super-finishing operation takes about 0.2 to 0.5 minutes. As in lapping and honing the high quality of surface obtained in super-finishing is due to:

1. Low specific pressure of the abrasive stone on the work surface.
2. Low cutting speeds.
3. Oscillation of the abrasive sticks.
4. Low temperatures generated.

5. Combination of oscillation and traverse movement bringing new cutting grains in contact with the workpiece and at the same time removing chipped material away from scene be excessive coolant.

Automobile parts that are super-finished can be listed as tappet, crankshaft, brake drum, pressure, plate, tappet body, camshaft, main bearing etc.

5.6 Burnishing

The burnishing of metals is a method for producing smooth surface by plasticall moving away the raised micro-irreguarities on the surface and pressing it into the micro-cavities. This produces a new surface with a high degree of finish.

The process is carried out with a highly polished ball or rolle type tool which is reversed under pressure over a rotating workpiece. When the tool strats the operation it produces a profile similar to ball curvature. With the feed given to the tool after one revolution the tool plastically metal deforms more metal. A small amount of the previous metal springs back. Both the deformation and springing back of metal continue with more and more feed given to the tool. In the end of tool traverse, it results into a smooth finished surface.

The quality of the surface produced depends upon the ball diameter, force, method of force application and, the hardness of the material. The improvement of the surface may range between 4 μ to 10 μ. The earlier condition of the surface also plays an important role achieved by this method.

5.7 BUFFING

Buffing is a polishing operation in which the workpiece is brought in contact with a revolving cloth buffing wheel, that usually has been charged with a very fine abrasive Fig. 5.13. The polishing action in buffing is very closely related to lapping in that when a polishing medium such as 'rouge' is used, the cloth buffing wheel becomes a carrying vehicle for the fine abrasives. In this action the abrasive removes amounts of metal from the workpiece, thus eliminating the scratch marks and producing a very smooth surface. When softer metals are buffed, particularly without the use of an abrasive, there is some indication that a small amount of metal flow may occur which helps to reduce the high spots and produce a high polish.

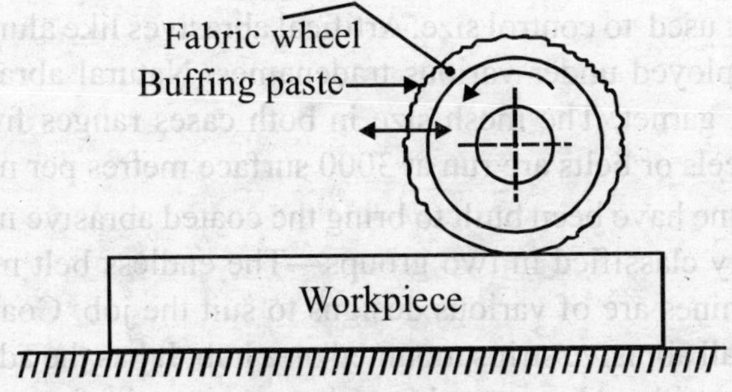

Fig. 513: Buffing

Buffing wheels are made of discs of linen, cotton, broad cloth and canvass. They are made more or less firm by the amount of stitching used to fasten the layers of the cloth together. Buffing wheels for very soft polishing or which can be used to polish into interior comers may have no stitching, the cloth layers being kept in position by the centrifugal force resulting from the rotation of the wheel. Buffing wheel speeds are in the range of 32.5 to 40 m/s.

Various types of buffing rouges are available. Most of them being primarily ferric oxide in some soft type of binder. Buffing should be used only to remove very fine scratches or to remove oxide or similar coatings which may be on the work surface. It ordinarily, is done manually, the work being held against the rotating wheel. This procedure is apt to be relative expensive because of labour cost. There are semi-automatic buffing machines available consisting of a series of individually driven buffing wheel which can be adjusted to the desired position so as to buff different portions of the workpiece. Workpieces are held in fixtures on a rotating circular work table so as to move past the buffing wheels. If the workpieces are not too complex in shape, very satisfactory results can be achieved with such equipment and the buffing cost will be low.

Buffing is used to give a much higher reflective finish than can be obtained by polishing. For a mirror like finish, the surface must be free from defects and deep scratches. Here also, the abrasive mixed in the lubricating binder is aluminium oxide. A colouring operation that brings out the best colour and lustre to the metal is done by using a white compound of alumina type abrasive.

Buffing wheels are mounted generally on buffing lathes or simply buffing machines which are run by belt drives from motors at the back. Wheels are mounted on both sides on such machine. Buffing speeds are little higher than polishing *i.e.*, 4000 m/min however, surface speeds of 2500 m/min should never be exceeded for colour buffing.

Product applications of buffing process which produces mirror like finish are the objects used on mobile homes, automobiles, motor cycles, boats, bicycles, supporting items, tools, store, fixtures, commercial and residential hardware and household utensils and appliances.

5.8 POLISHING PROCESS

Polishing is the smoothening of a surface by cutting action of abrasive particles adhered to the surfaces of resilient wheels of wood, felt, leather, canvas or fabric or attached to belts operating on resilient wheels. Polishing of metal is done to impart a high grade finish to the surface for the sake of appearance. Polishing is not used to control size. Artifical abrasives like aluminum oxide and silicon carbide are commonly employed under various tradenames. Natural abrasives can also be used. These are flint, emery and garnet. The mesh size in both cases ranges from 12 to 400. For best results in polishing the wheels or belts are run at 3000 surface metres per minute.

Many kinds of machnine have been built to bring the coated abrasive in contact with the work-piece. They may be broadly classified in two groups—The endless belt machines and the coated abrasive wheels. Belt machines are of various designs to suit the job. Coated abrasive wheels are made up of hundreds of small abrasive strips mounted on a hub. It has the advantages of conforming to a wide variety of contours without having to be made to any special form. The abrasives coated on a resilient surface cushioned by their own flexibility.

5.9 PICKLING AND OXIDIZING

Pickling refers to the removal of surface oxides, and scale from metals by acid solutions. Common pickling solutions contain sulphuric or hydrochloric acids and water and sometimes inhibitors which have been developed to reduce the harmful action of the acid fumes on plant equipment. Nitric and hydroflouric acids are used for some applications. In pickling, the parts must be perfectly cleaned before they are immersed in acid solution. After pickling, the parts must be rinsed and completely neutralized by an alkaline rinse, otherwise any trace of acid will corrode the material and harm paint or other subsequent coating.

Pickling is commonly done onrolled shapes, wires, sheets, heat-treated steel parts, wrought and cast aluminium parts. In some applications, such as on aluminium, pickling is called *oxidizing*.

5.10 ELECTROPLATING

Electroplating is the most popular means of applying metallic coatings on the surfaces of metals and sometimes on non-metals. This is done for protection against corrosion or against wear and abrasion, for appearance, to re-work worn parts by increase in size, to make pieces easy to solder and to stop off areas on steel parts from being carburized during heat treatment. Common plating metal are chromium, nickel, copper, zinc, cadmium, and tin. The more precious metals-silver, gold, platinum; and rhodium are also applied by plating.

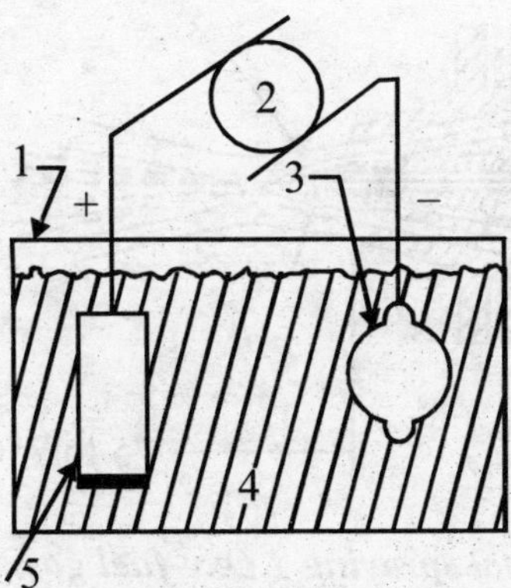

Fig. 5.14: Electroplating l. Plating tank. 2. D. C. source, 3. Workpiece, 4. Solution, 5. Anode (plating metal)

Surfaces to be plated must be buffed smooth to eliminate scratches and unevenness. The work is then cleaned in suitable cleaning solutions to remove all grease, dirt, buffing compound, etc. After rinsing, the part is ready for plating.

The four essential elements of a plating process are the cathode, anode, electrolyte, and direct current. They are shown in Fig. 5.14. The current leaves the anode, which is a bar of plating metal, and migrates through the electrolyte (water solution of salts of the metal to be applied) to the cathode, or part to be plated. As the ions are deposited on the cathode, they give up their charge and are deposited as metal on the cathode. Parts to be plated should be designed with generous fillets and radii instead of sharp corners, since current concentration occur at sharp points, resulting in excessive deposits.

5.11 HOT DIPPING GALVANIZING

A protective coating may be applied on metal pieces by dipping them into certain molten metals namely zinc, tin, or an alloy of lead and tin. Dipping is an economical way of putting on a heavy and enduring coating.

To obtain an even coating on small objects such as nuts, bolts, pins and washers, the objects are centrifuged, after being taken from the molten bath, until the coating is hard.

Zinc dipping, or hot galvanizing, is widely used on steel as an effective protection against corrosion. The parts are first cleaned and fixed in a solution of zinc chloride and hydrochloric acid.

5.12 METAL SPRAYING

Metal spraying is basically intended to confer some physical property on a surface. The appearance of poor surfaces on castings can be improved by metal spraying. Sprayed metal can be decorative, like aluminium or bronze on cast iron. Some can even be coloured.

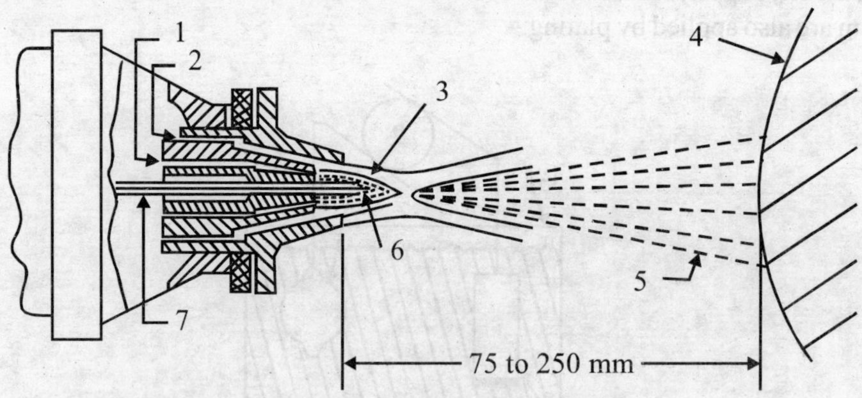

Fig. 5.15: Metal spraying 1.Oxy-fuel gas, 2. Compressed air, 3. Flame, 4. Workpiece, 5. Atomized spray, 6, Melting, 7. Wire.

Metal spraying is done by melting a metal in an oxy-gas flame and blowing it from the nozzle of a spray gun. In most guns the metal in the form of wire is fed by powered rollers to the flame, but some guns use powder or granulated metal. The process uses compressed air to atomize fully the molten metal or oxides and project them against a prepared surface where they are embedded, assuring good mechanical adhesions. This is illustrated in Fig 5.15. The surface must be roughened first and be free of dirt, oil and grease. The compressed air helps cool the work parts, so that the coatings may be applied successively not only to metals but also to glass, wood, asbestos, and certain plastics.

A metal spary gun may be directed by hand or mounted on a machine.

5.13 METALLISATION

Metallisation is an interesting application of the oxy-acetylene flame. This technique essentially consists in laying deposits which vary both in nature and in thickness, on to the widest variety of parts.

The principle is as follows: the material to be deposited is melted in a flame and subsequently pulverised and sprayed in fine droplets on to the part to be coated. The equipment used is a gun. It comprises a special torch, coupled with a compressed air pulverising device and a system of feeding the product.

Any product can be sprayed: metal, ceramics, plastics, on to any metal, and under certain conditions on to many non-metallic supports: wood, plaster, plastics, etc, Metallised surfaces laid in a thin layer of from 40 to 200 microns (zinc and aluminium) provide a much stronger and longer lasting protection against corrosion than any other more or less composite film.

REVIEW QUESTIONS

1. Explain the importance of surface finish.
2. Name and explain the various elements of surface roughness.
3. What is meant by 'Primary texture' and 'Secondary texture'.
4. What is meant by 'Lay'? Enumerate the various types of Lay and give the symbol for each.
5. Describe the process of Hand Lapping.
6. Give the units of surface roughness.
7. How surface roughness is represented?
8. Discuss the various methods of measurement of surface roughness.
9. How lapping and boning differ?
10. What are the purposes of lapping and honing?
11. Briefly explain the process of lapping.
12. Briefly explain the process of honing.
13. Discuss two general types of honing machines.
14. What is the difference between lapping and honing?
15. Briefly express the process of buffing.
16. Give the product applications of lapping, honing and buffing process.
17. State the merits and demerits of honing and give some applications of this process.
18. What is super-finishing? How does it differ from lapping and honing?
19. How is super-finishing done?
20. Discuss the effects of surface quality on functional properties. Give the factors affecting surface finish.
21. With the help of a neat diagram describe the process of super-finishing.
22. Name the common abrasives used in 'lapping' and 'honing' process.
23. Write short notes on the following:
    (*a*) Polishing. (*b*) Buffing.
    (*c*) Tumbling. (*d*) Burnishing.

Chapter 6

Jigs and Fixtures

6.1 IMPORTANCE AND USE OF JIGS AND FIXTURES

The jigs and the fixtures are the economical means to produce repetitive type of works by incorporating special work holding and tool guiding devices. The following are the advantages of employing jigs and fixtures in mass production work:

(1) It, eliminates the marking out; measuring, and other setting methods [illegible]

(2) It increases the machining accuracy, because the workpiece is automatically located and the tool is guided without making any manual adjustment.

(3) It enables production of identical parts which are inter-changeable. This facilitates the assembly operation.

(4) It increases the production capacity by enabling a number of workpieces to be machined in the single set up, and in some cases a number of tools may be made to operate simultaneously. The handling time is also greatly reduced due to quick setting and locating of the work. The speed, feed and depth of cut for machining can be increased due to high clamping rigidity of jigs and fixtures.

(5) It reduces the operator's labour and consequent fatigue as the handling operations are minimised and simplified.

(6) It enables semi-skilled operator to perform the operations as the setting operation of the tool and the work are mechanised. This saves labour cost.

(7) It reduces the expenditure on the quality control of the finished products.

(8) It reduces the overall cost of machining by fully or partly automatising the processes.

6.1.1 Jig

A jig may be defined as a device which holds and locates a workpiece and guides and controls one or more cutting tools. The holding of the work and guiding of the tool are such that they are located in true positions relative to each other, In construction, a jig comprises a plate, a structure, or box made of metal or in some cases of non-metal having provisions for holding the components in identical positions one after the other, and, then guiding the tool in correct position on the work in accordance with the drawing, specification, or operation layout.

6.1.2 Fixture

A fixture may be defined as a device which holds and locates a workpiece during an inspection or for, a manufacturing operation, The fixture does not guide the tool. In construction, the fixtures comprise different standard or specially designed work-holding devices, which are clamped on the machine table to hold the work in position. The tools are set at the required positions on the work by using gauges or by manual adjustment. The following are the fundamental differences between a fixture with a jig.

(1) A fixture holds and positions, the work but does not guide the tool, whereas a jig holds, locates and as well as guides the tool.

(2) The fixtures are generally heavier in construction and are bolted rigidly on the machine table, whereas the jigs are made lighter for quicker handling, and clamping with the table is often unnecessary.

(3) The fixtures are employed for holding work in milling, grinding, planing; or turning operations, whereas the jigs are used for holding the work and guiding the tool particularly in drilling, reaming or tapping operations:

6.2 PRINCIPLES OF JIGS AND FIXTURES DESIGN

The successful designing of a jig or a fixture depends upon the analysis of several factors which must be carefully studied before the actual work is taken in hand. The following are the essential factors which must be considered in designing a jig or a fixture:

(i) Study of the component

(2) Study of the type and capacity of the machine.

(3) Study of the locating elements.

(4) Study of the loading and unloading arrangement.

(5) Study of the clamping arrangement.

(6) Study of the power devices for operating the clamping elements.

(7) Study of the clearance required between the jig and the component.

(8) Study of the indexing devices.

(9) Study of the tool guiding and cutter setting elements.

(10) Study of the fool-proofing arrangement.

(11) Study of the ejecting devices.

(12) Study of the swarf removal arrangement.

(13) Study of the rigidity and vibration problem.

(14) Study of the table fixing arrangement.

(15) Study of the safety devices.

(16) Study of the methods of manufacture of the jig base, body or frame.

6.2.1 Component

The actual component or the workpiece should be procured and studied for deciding the sequence of operations to be performed and evaluating the other designing details of the jigs or the fixtures. One of the work surface is machined to act as the datum surface from which all other measurements are taken.

6.2.2 The Machine

The proper selection of the machine is essential to enable it to perform operations required on the work. The knowledge of the important particulars like the machine capacity, size of the table, maximum length of travel of the tool or the work for feed movement, power input and other details of the machine must be available before commencing the design work.

6.3 LOCATION

The location refers to the establishment of a desired relationship between the workpiece and the jig or fixture. Correct location influences the accuracy of the finished products. The jigs and the fixtures are so designed that all possible movements of the component must be restricted. The determination of the locating points and clamping of the workpiece serve to restrict the movements of the component in any direction, while setting it at the correct position relative to the jig. The locating points are determined by first finding out the possible degrees of freedom of the workpiece, which are then restrained by suitable arrangements which serve as locators. The principle of determining locating points are described below.

6.3.1 Principle of Locations

As illustrated in Fig 6.1, a rectangular block is free to move along the axis *AB*, *CD* and *EF*. The body can also rotate about these axis, and thus the total degrees of freedom of a body along which it can move is six. In order to locate the block correctly within a jig, all these six movements must be restrained by arranging suitable locating points and then clamping the block in position. The principles of determining locating points of certain typical objects are described below.

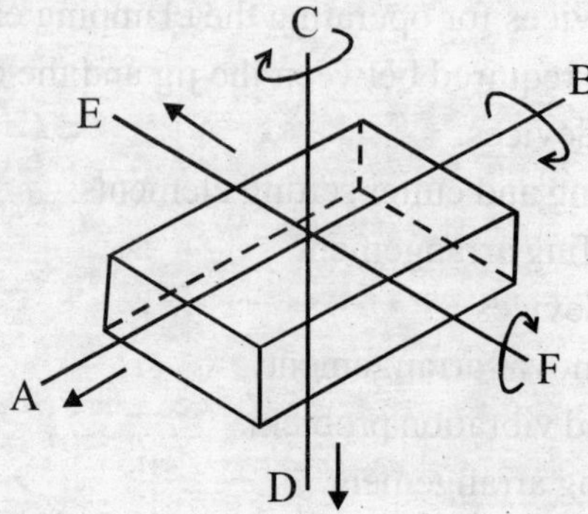

Fig. 6.1: Six degree freedom of a rectangular block.

6.3.2 Six Point Location of a Rectangular Block

It is assumed that the block in the Fig. 6.1 is made to rest on several points on the jig body as shown in Fig. 6.2. The bottom of the block is supported against three points, the rear, face of the block bears against two points and the side of the block rests against a single point, all projecting from the jig body. It will be now clear that the downward movement of the block along *CD* is restrained by three supporting points, which have the capability of supporting even a rough casting, The movements along *EF* and *AB* axis are restrained by the double and the single points respectively. The rotary movements of the block about *AB*, *CD* and *EF* axis are also restrained by the bottom back and side pins. The six points thus serve to locate a block correctly while restraining all its movements. The locating points for an uneven object can be determined by different arrangements but the guiding principle remains the same.

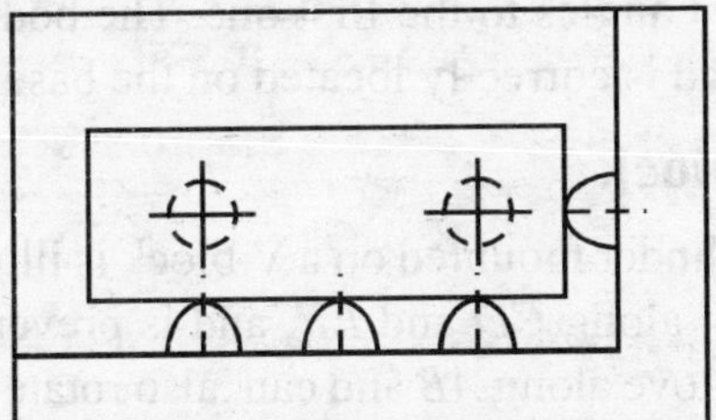
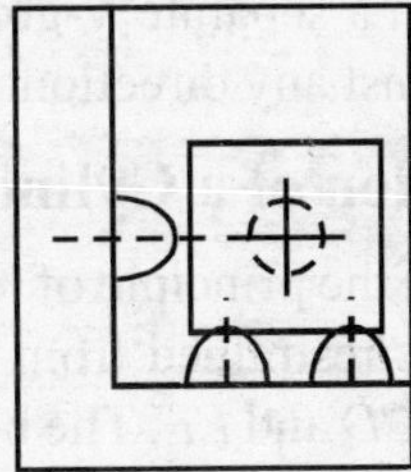

Fig. 6.2: Six location of a rectagular block.

6.3.3 Six Point Location of a Three Legged Object

The principle of locating a three legged object is illustrated in Fig 6.3 (A). The object is resting on three pointed legs on a flat surface. It is thus prevented from moving along *CD* and restrained from rotating along *EF* and *AB* axis. The *AB*, *CD* and *EF* refers to the axis as illustrated in Fig. 6.1. In the Fig. 6.3 (B), the front legs are made ball ended and are made to rest, on a V-groove. The spherical balls make a perfect mating surface with the V. The object is now restrained to move along *AB* and is prevented from rotation about *CD*. In the Fig. 6.3 (C), the rear leg is also made ball ended and is

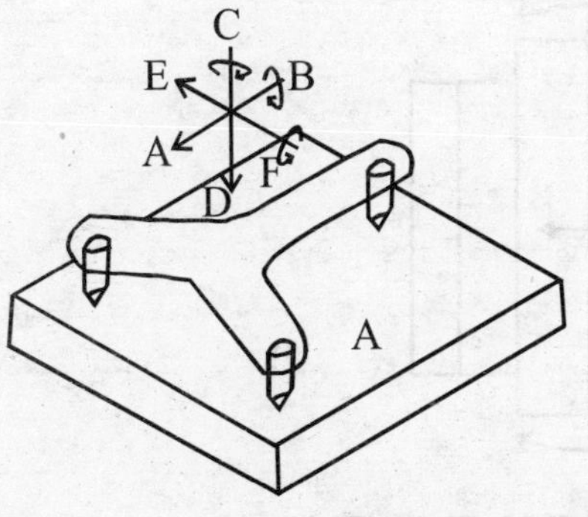

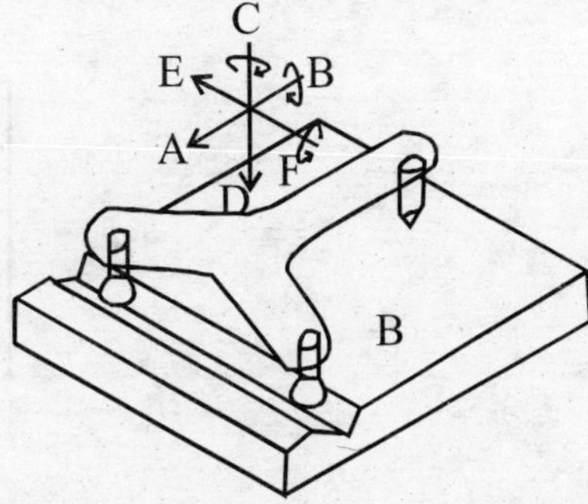

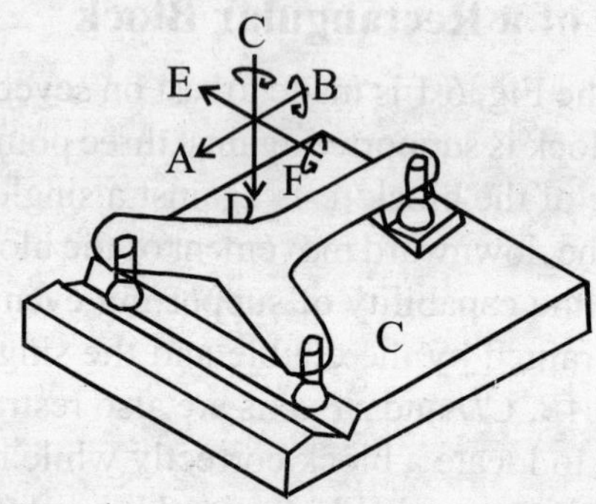

Fig. 6.3: Six point location of a three legged object

made to rest on a separate V-groove set at right angles to the first one. The body is now perfectly restrained against any directional movement and is correctly located on the base plate.

6.3.4 Location of a Cylinder on a V-block

The analysis of the principle of location of a cylinder mounted on a V-block is illustrated in Fig. 6.4. The cylinder is restrained from any movement along *CD* and *EF*, and is prevented from rotation about the axis *CD* and *EF*. The body is free to move along *AB* and can .also rotate about the axis *AB*. The free movements of the work are shown by dotted arrows. In order to locate the work completely, certain other locating arrangements must be incorporated in addition to the V-block.

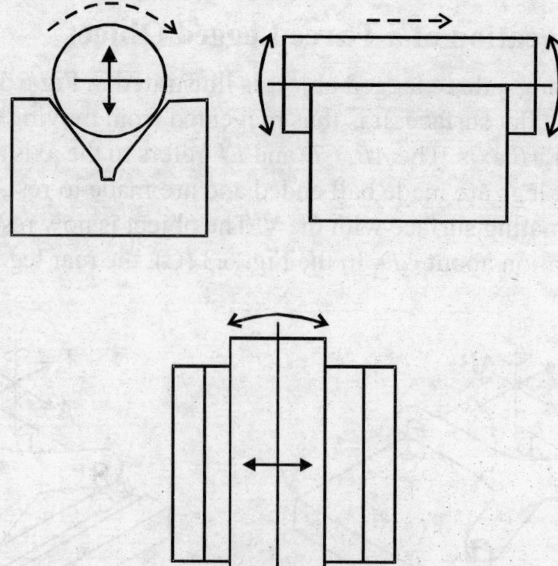

Fig. 6.4: Location of a cylinder on a V-block.

6.4 METHODS OF LOCATION

There are many different methods of locating a work. The locating arrangement required for a particular work is selected after studying the type of work, type of operation, degree of accuracy required, number of articles to be manufactured and many other factors. The different locating methods are described below.

6.4.1 Flat Locator

The flat type locators illustrated in Fig. 6.5 are employed for locating flat machined faces of the component. In Fig 6.5 (A) the component is bearing directly on the machined face of the jig body. An undercut is provided at the bottom for swarf clearance. The flat headed button type locators, fitted on the jig body, are illustrated in Fig. 6.5 (B) and (C). The button type locators are superior in action than plain flat locators. The poisoning of the button illustrated in (B) is a better arrangement than in. (C) due to its capacity to take end load and for having provision of swarf clearance. The button in (C) may be bent due to the end pressure.

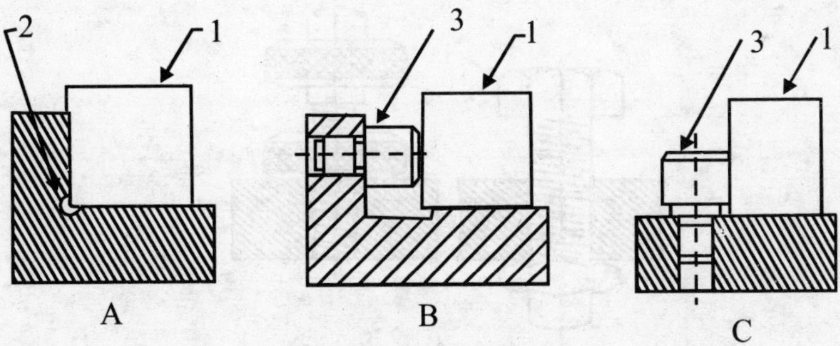

Fig. 6.5: Flat locators
(A) Location by jig body, (B) Location by button,
(C) Location by button 1. Work, 2. Undercut, 3. Button.

6.4.2 Cylindrical Locator

The cylindrical locator illustrated in Fig. 6.5 (D) is employed for locating components having drilled holes. The cylindrical locator fitted on the jig body is inserted in the drilled hole of the component to locate it in position. The face of the jig body around the locator is undercut to provide space for swarf clearance. When two holes on the component serve to locate it, one of the button head is flattened to compensate for any slight inaccuracy in the centre distance between the two drilled holes in the component.

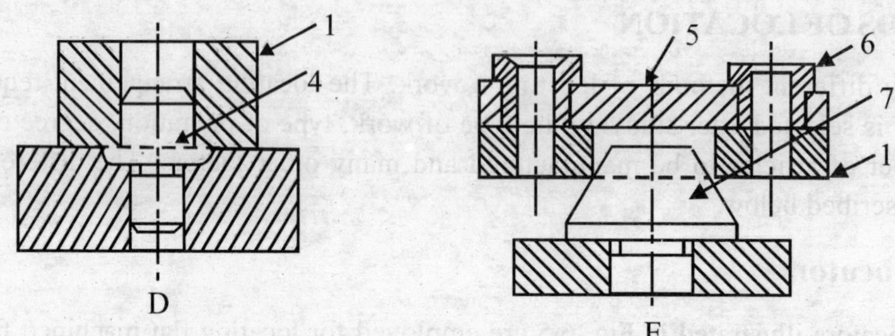

Fig. 6.5 (D) Cylindrical locator (1. Work, 4. Cylindrical locator).
(E) Conical locator (1. Work, 5. Template, 6. Drill bush, 7. Conical locator).

6.4.3 Conical Locator

The conical locator illustrated in Fig. 6.5 (E) is used for locating workpieces having drilled holes. The conical locator is superior to a pin locator due to its capacity to accommodate a slight variation in the hole diameter of the component without affecting the accuracy of the location.

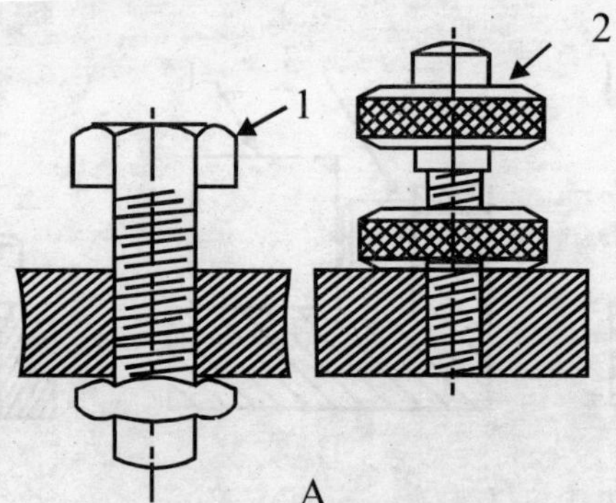

Fig. 6.6 (A) Jack pin locator
1. Bolt head type, 2. Knurled knob type).

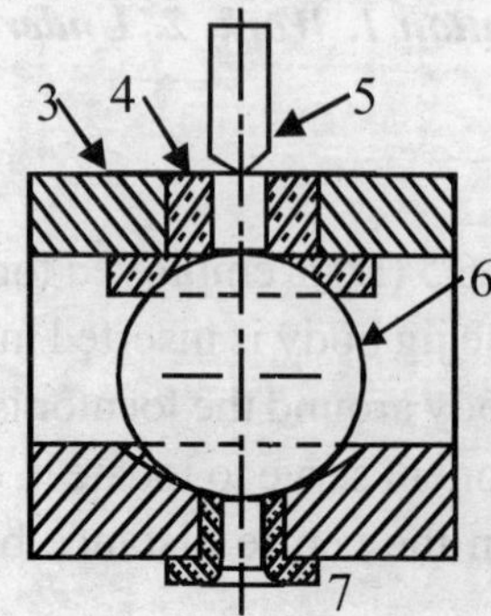

Fig. 6.6 (B) Drill bush locator 3. jig body,
4. Drill bush locator, 5. Drill, 6. Work, Drill bush).

6.4.4 Jack Pin Locator

The jack pin locator illustrated in Fig. 6.6 (A) is employed for supporting rough workpieces from the bottom, while locating it. The height of the pins are adjustable to accommodate the variation in the surface texture of several components, which ate rough and unmachined.

6.4.5 Drill Bush Locator

The drill bush locator illustrated in Fig. 6.6 (B) is employed for locating cylindrical workpieces. The bush has conical opening for locating purpose and is sometimes screwed on the jig body for adjustment of height of the work. The drill bush also serves the purpose of guiding the tool.

6.4.6 Fixed V-locator

The fixed V-locator, illustrated in Fig. 6.7 (A), is used to locate workpieces having circular or semicircular profiles. After setting the work, the V-block is clamped on the jig body by screws, and positioned by dowels. The V-groove is made slightly tapered for clamping purposes. The standard included angle of the V -block is 90° degrees.

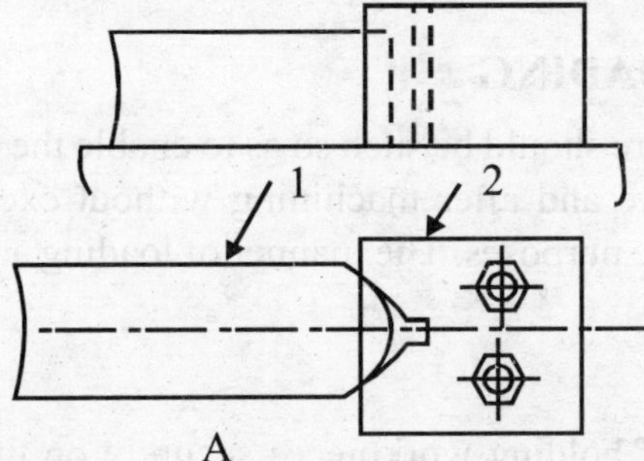

Fig. 6.7 (A): Fixed V-locator 1. Work, 2. Fixed V-block

6.4.7 Sliding V-locator

The sliding V-locator, illustrated in Fig.6.7 (B), is used in conjunction with fixed V-locators for locating workpieces having circular or semicircular profiles. Thee work is quickly located by adjusting the position of the sliding V-block 3 within its body 2, by rotating the knob 4 of the, threaded spindle. A circular flange integral with the threaded spindle contacts a slot at the underside of the V-block 3, and the movement of the screw is communicated to the V-block through this flange.

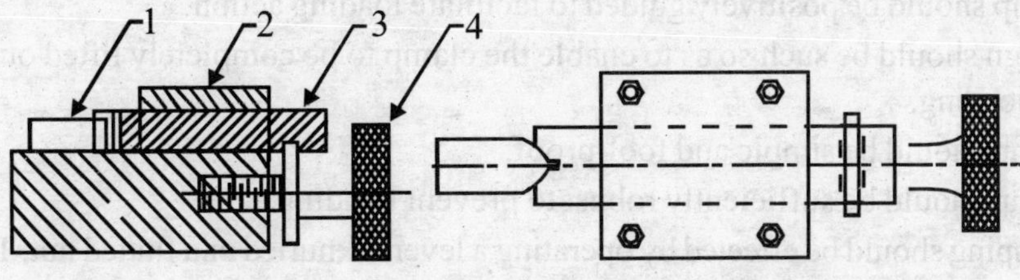

Fig. 6.7 (B): Sliding V-locator 1. Work, 2. Jig body, 3. Sliding V-block, 4. Knurled knob

6.4.8 Outside Pin Locator

The outside pin locator illustrated in Fig. 6.7 (C), is used to locate a work having odd, irregular profiles. The pins or the buttons are arranged on the jig body, following a contour corresponding to the outside profile of the work.

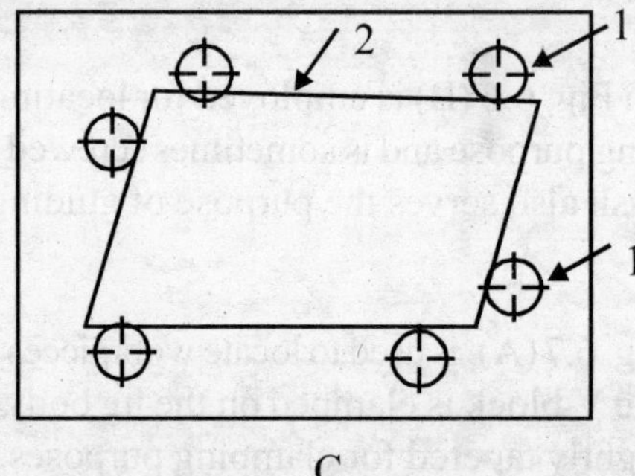

Fig. 6.7 (C): Outside pin locator 1. Pin, 2. Work

6.5 LOADING AND UNLOADING

The design of the jig and the fixture should be such so as to enable the operator to fix up and remove the components with ease, before and after machining without exerting unnecessary effort and spending undue idle time for these purposes. The manner of loading and unloading should be quick, simple and positive.

6.6 CLAMPING

The clamps serve the purpose of holding workpieces securely on the jigs or fixtures against the cutting forces. In order to achieve the most efficient clamping, the following operational factors must be considered.

(1) The clamping pressure should be exerted on the solid supporting part of the work to prevent distortion.

(2) The clamping pressure should be kept low. It should be sufficient to hold the work against the cutting pressure.

(3) The movement of the clamp for loading and unloading purposes should be kept limited.

(4) The clamp should be positively guided to facilitate loading action.

(5) The design should be such so as to enable the clamp to be completely lifted out of the work, while unloading.

(6) The clamp should be simple and fool-proof.

(7) The clamp should be sufficiently robust to prevent bending.

(8) The clamping should be effected by operating a lever, a knurled or a flutted nut. The haxagonal headed nuts or bolts should be avoided as far as practicable to eliminate the use of spanners. If it becomes essential to use hexagonal nuts; only one size spanner should be used throughout.

(9) The clamps should be case-hardened to prevent wear of the clamping faces.
(10) The clamps should be so arranged on the work to perform as many operations as possible in one setting.
(11) The clamping parts should be designed to make it non-detachable from the jig.

6.7 TYPES OF CLAMPS

The following are the different types of clamps, which are commonly used with jigs and fixtures:

(1) Screw clamp	(2) Flat clamp	(3) Pivoted clamp
(4) Equalising clamp	(5) Latch clamp	(6) Swing-plate clamp
(7) Double acting clamp.	(8) Wedge clamp	(9) Cam clamp

6.7.1 Screw Clamp

The screw clamp, illustrated in Fig. 6.8 (A), is used to grip the work on its edges. This type of clamping arrangement enables the top surface of the work to be machined without any difficulty. Though the clamping method is quite simple, it possesses the following defects:

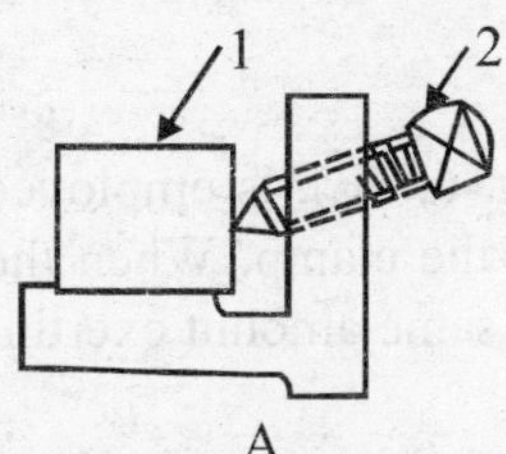

Fig. 6.8 (A) Screw clamp 1. Work, 2. Screw

(1) Longer time is required for clamping or unclamping the work.
(2) The clamping force changes from the component to component.
(3) Large effort is required to clamp a work.
(4) Indentation marks are left on the edges of the work by the pointed ends of the screws.

6.7.2 Flat Clamp

The flat clamp illustrated in Fig. 6.8 (B) supports the work by the clamp face, which is pressed against the work by tightening the nut. There are several types of flat clamps.

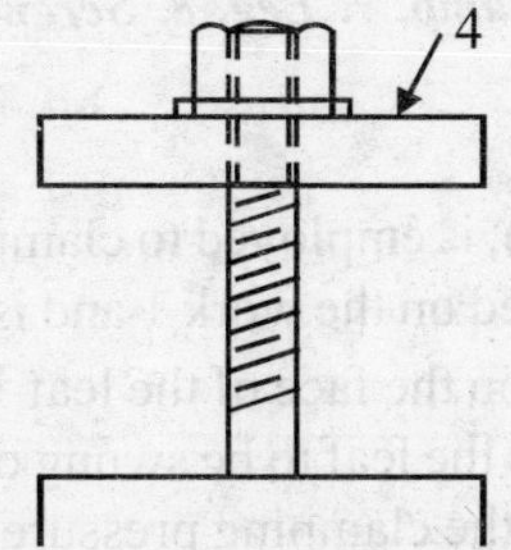

Fig. 6.8 (B): Flat clamp 4. Strap

6.7.3 Pivoted Clamp

The pivoted clamp illustrated in Fig. 6.8 (C) eliminates the use of spanner for clamping purposes. The work 1 can be gripped quickly by rotating the screw 5; which actuates a pivoted clamp 4 on the face of the work. The springs illustrated in Fig. 6.8 (D) guide the clamp of the same type in horizontal position when the work is unloaded.

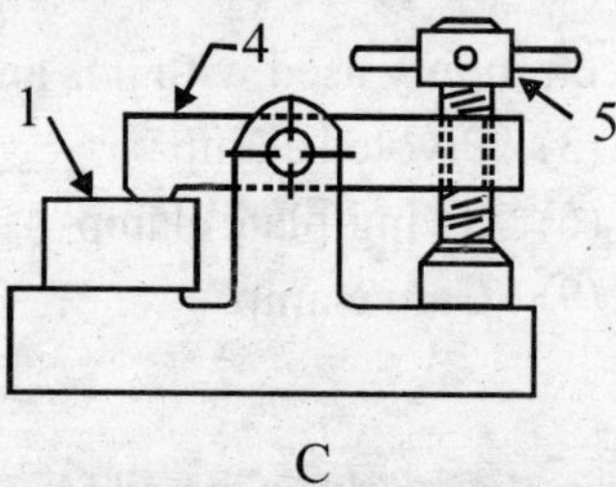

Fig. 6.8 (C) Pivoted clamp
1. Work, 4. Strap, 5. Screw.

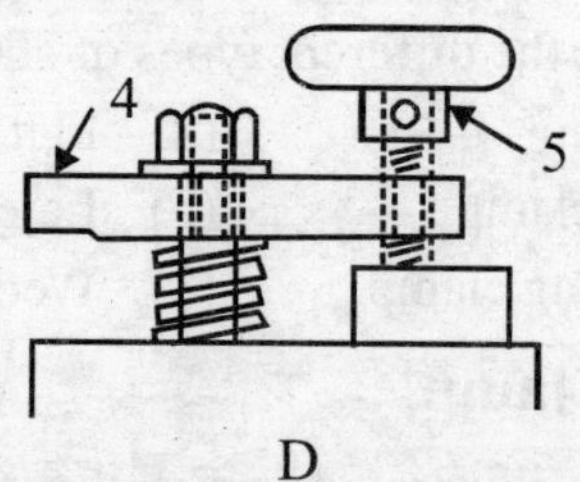

Fig. 6.8 (D) Pivoted clamp
4. Strap, 5. Screw.

6.7.4 Equalising Clamp

The equalising clamp, illustrated in Fig. 6.8(E), is employed to exert equal pressure on the two faces of the work by the two legs 7 of the clamp. When the screw 8 is rotated, the two legs of the clamp press against the work by the same amount exerting equal pressure on its two clamping surfaces.

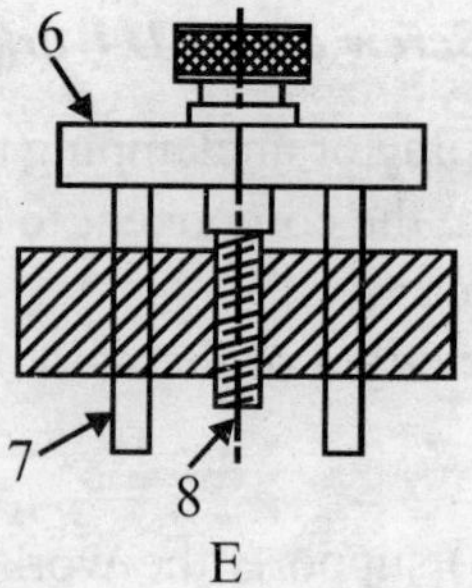

Fig. 6.8 (E): Equalising clamp
6. Clamp, 7. Leg, 8. Screw.

6.7.5 Latch Clamp

The latch clamp, illustrated in Fig. 6.8 (F), is employed to clamp a work by a latch and a pivoted leaf. As shown in the figure the leaf 12 is closed on the work 1 and is kept in position by the latch 10. The work 1 is gripped by the spring 11 fitted on the face of the leaf 12. To unload the work, the tailend of the latch 10 is pushed by hand that causes the leaf to be swung open, releasing the work. The loading and unloading arrangement is quick, but the clamping pressure is not very high in this device.

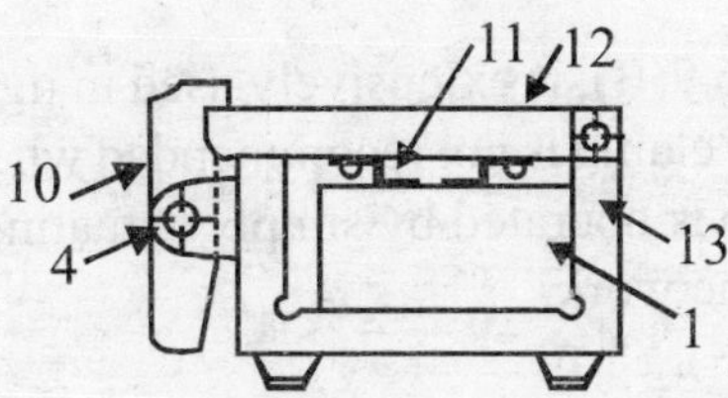

Fig. 6.8 (F): Latch clamp 1. Work, 4. Pivot, 10. Latch, 11. Leafspring, 12. Leaf, 13. Jig body.

6.7.6 Swing Plate Clamp

The swing plate clamps are employed for quick loading and unloading purposes on light jobs. A swing plate is illustrated in Fig. 6.8 (G). The clamp is operated by swinging the plate in position and locking it by turning a screw which passes through its centre.

Fig. 6.8 (G): Swing plate

6.7.7 Double Acting Clamp

The double acting clamp, illustrated in Fig. 6.8 (H), is employed to grip the work by rotating the central screw, which actuates the two clamps placed at the two sides of the work to operate simultaneously. Sufficient gripping pressure is applied by these clamps.

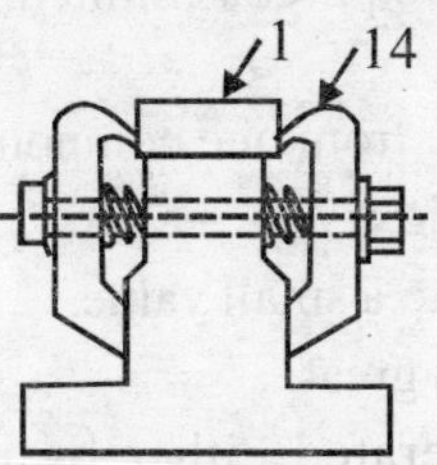

Fig. 6.8 (H): Double acting clamp 1. Work, 14. Clamp

6.7.8 Wedge Clamp

The wedge clamp, illustrated in Fig. 6.9 (A), is employed to grip the work 1 by the wedge block 3, which is made to slide by rotating the screws 4. The wedge block grips the work against the fixed button 2 fitted on the other end of the jig body.

6.7.9 Cam Clamp

The cam clamp, illustrated in Fig. 6.9(B), is extensively used in jig and fixture, work due to its rapid and convenient action. This type of clamp is not recommended where vibration is present, because it may slacken the clamp. The clamp is operated by simply actuating the handle 7 up or down which locks or unlocks the strap 6 with the work.

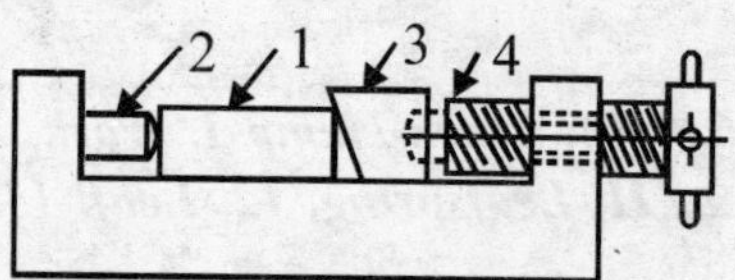

Fig. 6.9 (A): Wedge clamp 1. Wark, 2. Button, 3. Wedge, 4. Screw

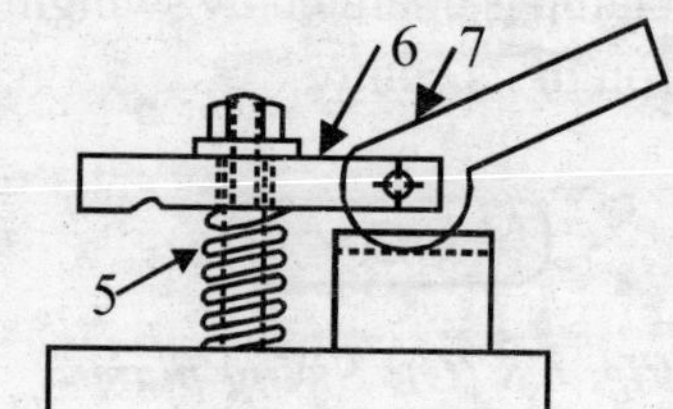

Fig. 6.9 (B): Cam clamp 1. Helical spring, 2. Strap, 3. Cam handle

6.8 POWER DEVICES FOR CLAMPING

The jig and fixture clamps are operated by hand or power. Hand clamping is employed in small components where the clamping pressure required is limited. The following are the disadvantages of hand clamping.

(1) The clamping pressure is variable from one component to the other.

(2) The operator's fatigue is inevitable.

(3) The clamping pressure is limited to a small value.

(4) The time required for clamping is great.

The power-driven clamps are operated either by pneumatic of hydraulic power. The power driven clamps are quick acting, controllable, reliable, and operated without least fatigue to the operator. The power clamps exert high clamping pressure and are employed for gripping heavy workpieces.

6.9 CLEARANCE IN A JIG AND FIXTURE

It is necessary to leave sufficient clearance between the jig body and the component to accommodate variable sizes of work which are manufactured either by casting or forging.

6.10 INDEXING ARRANGEMENT

The indexing arrangement is incorporated in a jig to enable operations to be performed on the periphery of a work at different angular positions by turning and setting the work at that position. Fig.6.9 illustrates an indexing arrangement. The work is mounted on the index plate spindle 4, and is kept in position by the spring loaded lever 2. After the first operation is complete, the lever 2 is pushed aside and then the index plate 3 with the work is turned to the requited angular position. The plate with the work is locked in position by the lever which engages with the desired slot of the index plate.

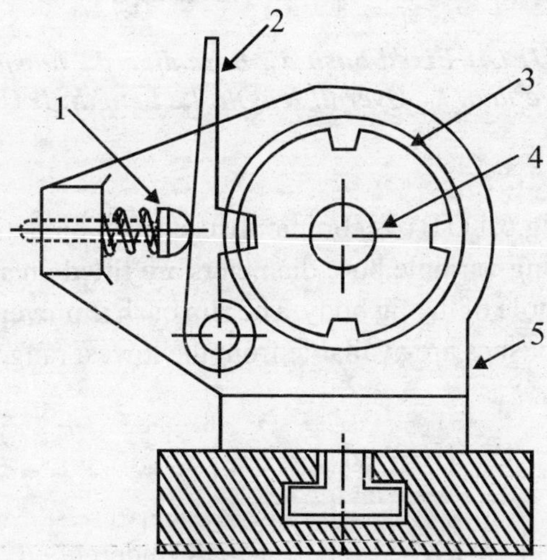

Fig. 6.10: Indexing Arrangement in Jigs
1. Spring loaded plunger, 2. Lever, 3. Index plate,
4. Index plate spingle,
5. Jig body

6.11 TOOL GUIDING AND CUTTER SETTING ARRANGEMENT

The cutter is set relative to the work in a fixture by adjusting the machine or by using the cutter setting block. The tools are guided in jigs by drill bushes which are fitted on the jig plates. There are three different types of jig bushes: fixed bush, slip bush, and liner bush.

6.11.1 Fixed Bush

The fixed bush, illustrated in Fig. 6.11 (A), fits directly into the jig plate and is used to guide the tool. The bush can guide only one tool and the life of the jig and the life of the bush is estimate to be same. The fixed bushes are available from the lowest range to the 63 mm of bore diameter and the length of the bush ranges from 6 to 36 mm.

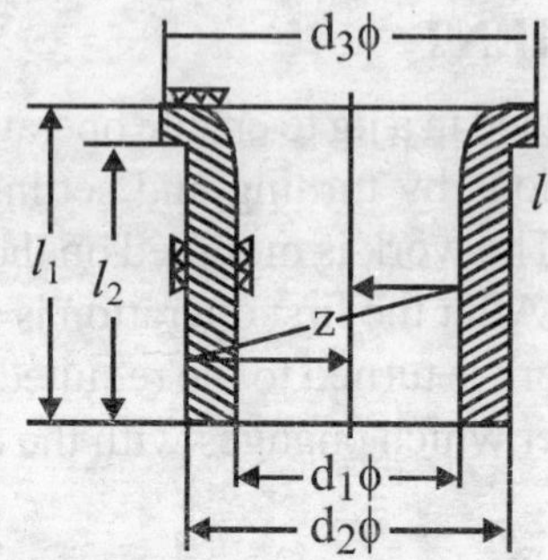

Fig. 6.11: (A) Fixed bush d_1. Bore dia., d_2. outside dia., d_3. Flange dia., l_1. Overall length, l_2. Length, l. Undercut.

6.11.2 Slip Bush

The slip bush, illustrated in Fig.6.11 (B), is commonly used in conjunction with a liner bush to guide the tool. The slip bushes having variable bore diameters are fitted on a liner bush to receive two or more tools through the same hole of the jig body. The slip bush is prevented from rotation by friction with the liner bush. The slip bushes are available from the lowest range to 48 mm of bore diameter.

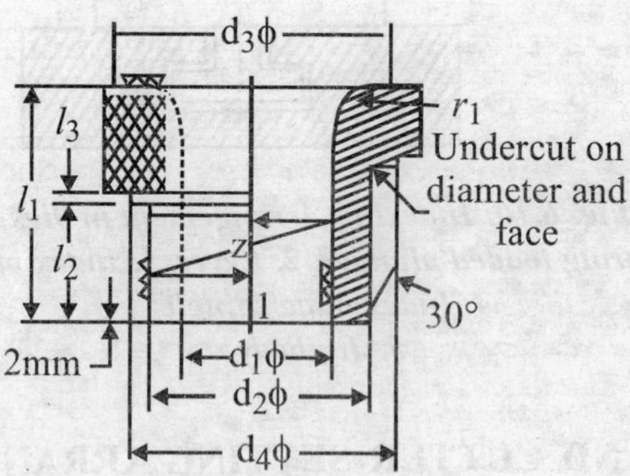

Fig. 6.11: (B) Slip Bush d_1, Bore dia., d_2, outside dia., d_3, Flange dia., d_4 Collar dia., 1_1, Overall length, 1_2, length

6.11.3 Liner Bush

The liner bush, illustrated in Fig. 6.11 (C), fits permanently into jig plate and receives the slip bush. The liner bush can also guide a tool independently. The bushes are available from the lowest range to the 63 mm of bore diameter.

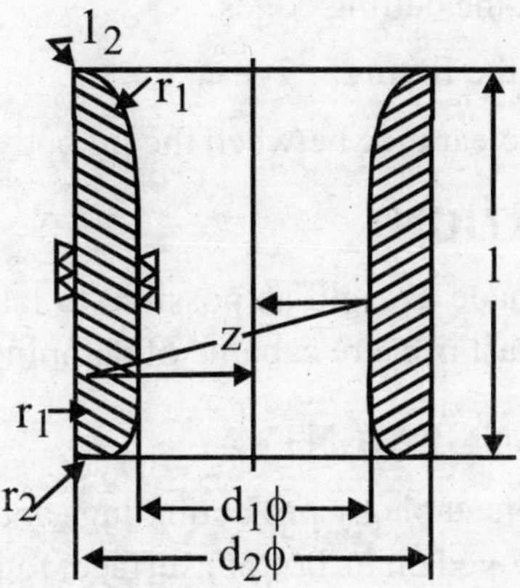

Fig. 6.11: (C) Liner Bush d_1. Bore dia., d_2. Outside dia., 1. Overall length

6.12 FOOL-PROOFING

The fool-proofing means designing of jig and fixture with such devices so as to make it impossible for an operator to insert a component into a jig or a fixture in any position other than the correct one. The arrangement prevents the accidental error of the operator from spoiling the work, The fool proofing is accomplished by using fouling pegs, cross frames, pins or abutments arranged within the jig, and they do not interfere with the correct location of the work.

6.13 EJECTION

The jigs and fixtures are designed to eject heavy workpieces mechanically when it is unclamped. This saves time and labour of the operator. The ejection of components are accomplished by wedges, spring loaded or cam actuated plun gers.

6.14 SWARF REMOVAL

The jigs and fixtures must be designed to have arrangements for swarf removal as the accumulation of swarf under the jig base or on the table can deform the work on clamping, affect the accuracy of location, and cause wastage in time if the swarf is removed by hand after each cut. The removal of chips from jigs and fixtures can be accomplished by the following methods.

(1) By designing the shape of the jig parts to enable the chips to fall out by gravity.

(2) By making holes in the jig body for swarf removal.

(3) By undercutting the corners to clear the work.

(4) By using raised supports or buttons for location.

(5) By applying air blast at the cutting edges of the tool.

(6) By applying air suction at the cutting edges.

(7) By using fixed wipers on the fixture.

(8) By maintaining marginal clearance between the jig body and the component.

6.15 RIGIDITY AND VIBRATION

The jigs and fixtures should be made as rigid as possible to take up the cutting load without any deformation. Bulky jigs made of cast iron are capable of damping vibration.

6.16 TABLE FIXING ARRANGEMENT

The jigs are attached on the machine table by projecting lugs and the fixtures are clamped by bolts. When the jigs are required to be moved on its bottom surface, four small raised portions are made to act as supports. These projections are called *jig feet*. The jig feet should be designed to allow the centre of gravity of the component and the jig to lie between the feet to impart it stability.

6.17 SAFETY DEVICES

The jigs and fixtures are designed to assure full safety to the operator. All sharp edges should be rounded and all revolving parts should be guarded against any possible injury.

6.18 TYPES OF JIGS

The quality, type, and complexity of jigs used depend solely on the type of work to be machined and the scale of production required. A few simple type of drill jigs are described below:

(1) Template jig

(2) Plate jig

(3) Channel jig

(4) Diameter jig

(5) Leaf jig

(6) Ring jig

(7) Box jig

6.18.1 Template Jig

The template jig is the simplest of all the types. A plate 2 having holes at the desired positions serves as a template which is fixed on the component 1 to be drilled The drill 21 is guided through these holes of the template 2 and the required holes are drilled on the workpiece at the same relative positions with each other as on the template. A template jig is illustrated in Fig. 6.12 (A).

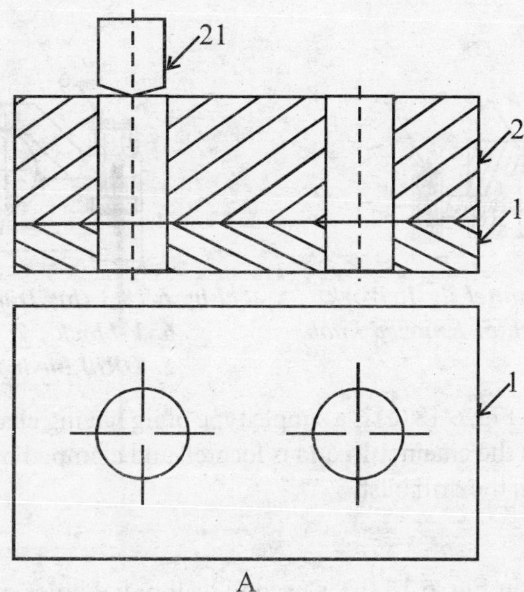

Fig. 6.18.1 (A): Template jig 1. Work, Template, 21. Drill

6.18.2 Plate Jig

A plate jig is an improvement of the template jig by incorporating drill bushes on the template. The plate jigs are employed to drill holes on large parts maintaining accurate spacing with each other. A plate jig is illustrated in Fig: 6.18.2 (B).

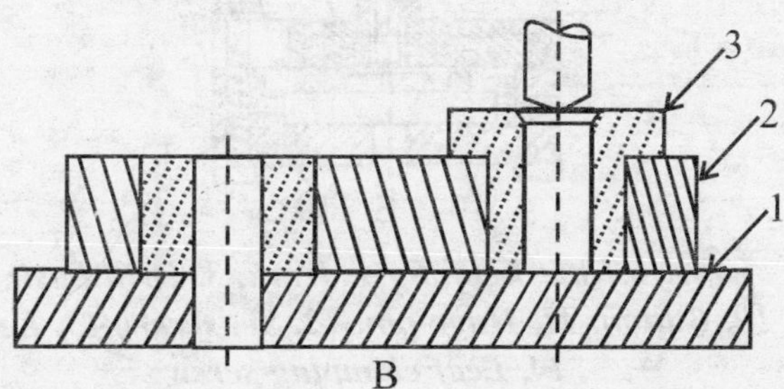

Fig. 6.18.2: Plate jig 1. Work, Template, 3. Drill bush

6.18.3 Channel Jig

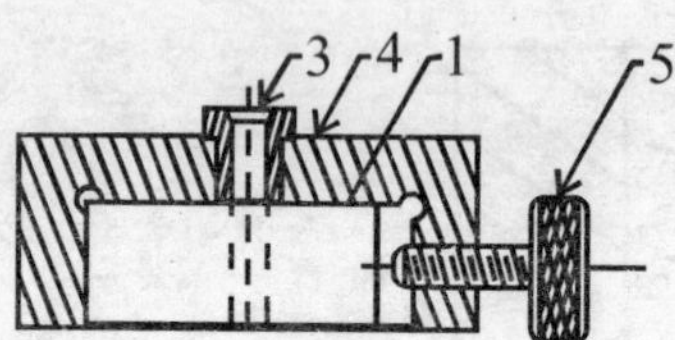

Fig. 6.18.3 (a): Channel jig 1. Work, Drill bush, 4. Channel, 5. Knurled knob.

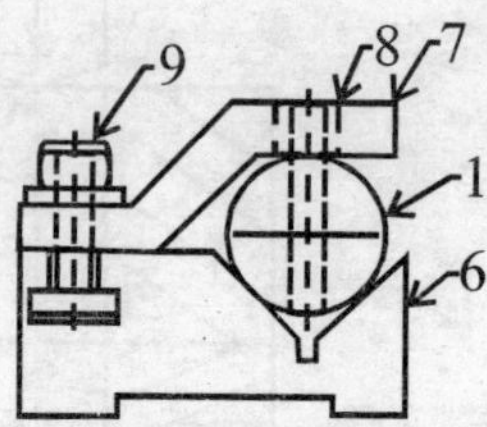

Fig. 6.18.3 (b): Diameter Jig 1. Work, 6. V-block , 7. Clamping plate, 8. DRill bush, 9. Clamping bolt.

The channel jig illustrated in Fig. 6.18 (a) is a simple type of jig having channel like cross-section. The component 1 is fitted within the channel 14 and is located and clamped by rotating the knurled knob 5. The tool is guided through the drill bush 3.

6.18.4 Diameter Jig

The diameter jig illustrated in Fig. 6.18 (b) is used to drill radial holes on a cylindrical or spherical workpieces. The work 1 is placed on the fixed V-block 6 and then, clamped by the clamping plate 7 which also locates the work. The tool is guided through the drill bush 8 which is set radially with the work.

6.18.5 Leaf Jig

The leaf, jig illustrated in Fig. 6.18.5 has a leaf or a plate 13 hinged on the body at 11 and the leaf may be swung open or closed on the work for loading or unloading purposes. The work 1 is located by the buttons 10 and is clamped by set screws 12. The drill bush 3 guides the toot:

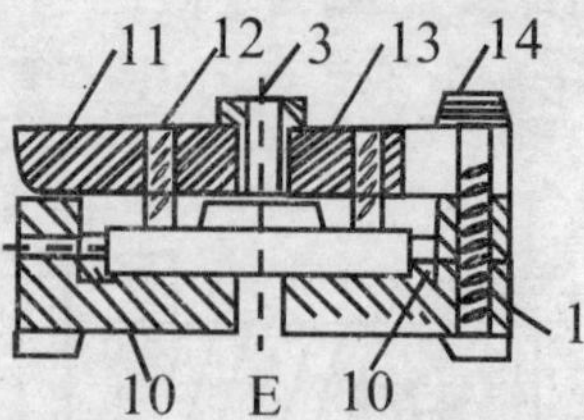

Fig. 6.18.5: Leaf Jig 1. Work, 3. Drill bush, 10. Button, 11. Huge pin, 12. Set screw, 13. Leaf, 14. Leaf clamping screw

6.18.6 Ring Jig

The ring jig illustrated in Fig. 6.12 (F) is employed to drill holes on circular flanged parts. The work is securely clamped on the drill body and the holes are drilled by guiding the tool through drill bushes..

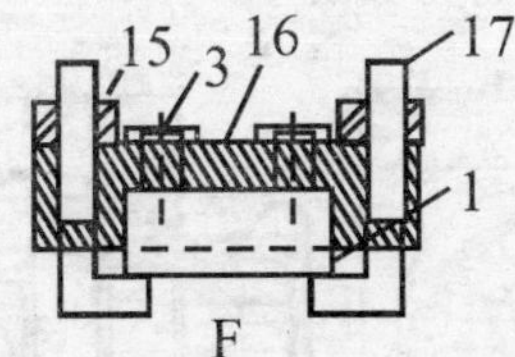

Fig. 6.18.6: Ring jig 1. Work, 3. Drill bush, 15. Nut, 16. Jig plate 17. Clamping bolt

6.18.7 Box Jig

The box jig illustrated in Fig. 6.18.7 is of box like construction within which the component is located by the buttons 18. The work 1 is clamped by rotating the can handle 19 which also locates it. The drill bush 3 guides the tool. The box jigs are generally employed to drill a number of holes on a component from different angles.

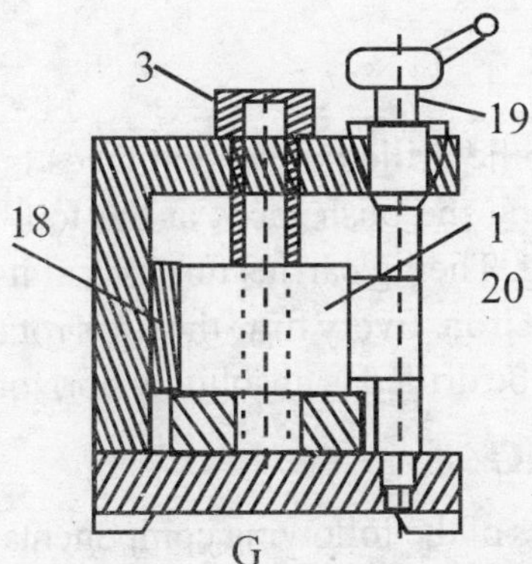

Fig. 6.18.7: Box jig 1. Work, 3. Drill bush, 18. Button, 19. Cam handle, 20. Cal

6.18.8 Index Jig

Such a Jig, Fig. 6.18.8, is used to drill a series of holes in a circle on the face of a workpiece. The workpiece is indexed and the next place where the hole is to be drilled, comes under the Jig bush. Indexing devices, to accomplish the indexing are discussed separately.

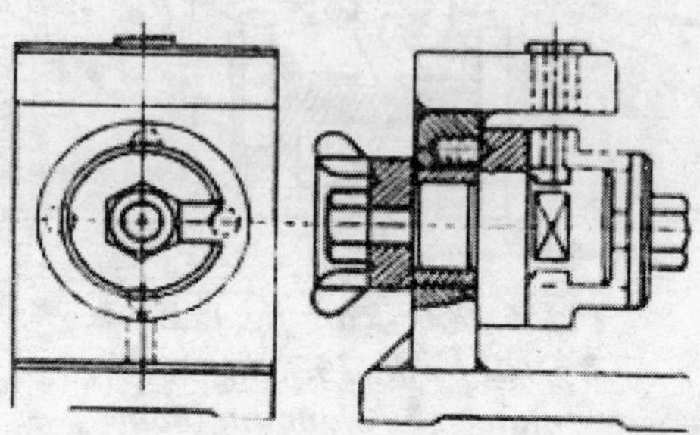

Fig. 6.18.8 : Index jig

6.18.9 Built-up Jig and Welded Jig

All types of Jigs mentioned so far can be made either be fabricated with the help of dowels and cap screws or by welding the plates and angles. Depending upon the mode of construction the jigs may be a built-up jig or a welded jig.

6.18.10 Trunion Jig

Heavy box Jigs where holes are to be drilled in several faces is moved on turnions instead of the operator tumbling them for bringing the bush faces at the top. Therefore a heavy jig moving on turnions is referred to as trunion jig. The jig carries turnions at its ends which rotate in cast bearing brackets mounted on a long channel iron. Every time the jig is rotated it must be locked in such a way that the face in which the hole is to be drilled is absolutely horizontal.

6.19 FIXTURE FOR MILLING

A milling fixture essentially consists of the following components built-up into the main base.

1. **Base:** The base of a fixture is about 20 to 25 mm thick, rigid enough not to deflect upward during upcut milling. It absorbs forces arising due to vibrational effects and chatter. Cast iron acts as an absorbent more efficiently than does fabricated steel base provided with lugs on each side for fixing the base to the machine table. Lug surfaces are slightly raised up and spot faced.
2. **Tenon strip:** The position of the base on the table is accurately located by means of tenon strips. The tenons identical in width with the slot in the machine table are fixed below the base. The length of a tenon strip is twice the width. They are made of ground and hardened steel. The tenon strip fixes the base of the fixture to machine table in the same relative position every time. These are held to the base with the help of screws. Fig. 6.14.

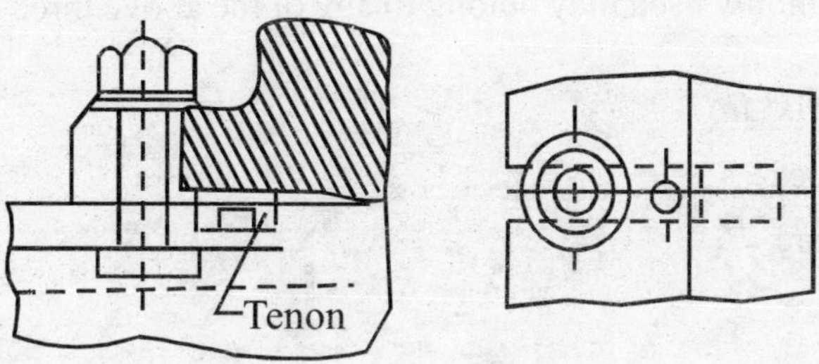

Fig. 6.19 (a)

3. **Setting Block:** Milling fixtures are provided with a setting block so that a feeler gauge of 0.02 mm thickness may be used for setting the fixture relative to the cutters. It is made of steel, duly hardened and ground. The setting piece is fixed to the base of fixture by means of screws and dowels. Fig. 6.19.(b)

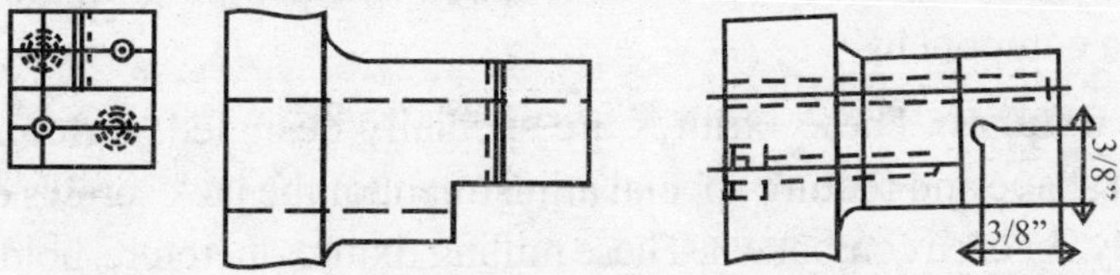

Fig. 6.19 (b): Ring jig 1. Work, 3. Drill bush, 15. Nut, 16. Jig plate 17. Clamping bolt

4. **Tee Bolts:** The fixture is bolted to the machine table with the bolts suitable for the slots provided in the machine table. The shank of the bolt goes into the lug and nut is tightened on the screwed portion.
5. **Clamping Device:** A fixture may have anyone of the clamping devices mentioned earlier to clamp the workpieces.
6. **Locating or Positioning Element:** The excessive thrust of the cutter must be resisted by a fixed stop because clamping device alone may not be sufficient.

6.19.1 Classification of Milling Fixtures

Milling fixtures can be classified in several ways: (1) Type of operations performed on the work, (2) Method of milling, (3) Method of clamping the workpiece.

According to the type of operations the fixtures may be classified as slotting, straddle milling, face milling or form milling fixtures. According to the method of milling the fixture may be named as a single piece milling fixture, string milling fixture, abreast milling fixture, reciprocal milling fixture, progressive milling fixture and index milling fixture. Third classification may identify the fixture as hand clamping fixture, power clamping fixtures or automatic clamping fixture. However, important types of fixture most commonly used may belong to any of the above three classes. Important types of fixtures are:

1. Special vice Jaw fixture
2. Plain milling fixture
3. String milling fixture
4. Gang milling fixture
5. Profile milling fixture
6. Continuous rotary milling
7. Indexing milling fixture

1. **Special vice Jaw fixtures:** A commonly used work holding device for milling is the plain or universal vice. Provision is made for attaching special jaw inserts to the fixed and movable vice jaws. Expenditure on special milling fixtures can often be avoided by carefully adopting special vice jaws, so formed as to provide location and clamping for either one or a series of operations on a component.

2. **Plain milling fixtures:** These fixtures are specially designed, for components which are complicated in shape and require special adjustment of the jack screws or spring loaded rest pins individually, for each component. These milling fixtures therefore, hold only one component because each component requires special attention. It is particularly true when first operation is performed on a forging or casting. The milled surface is to serve a datum for all other dimensions in subsequent operations. Therefore, the first surface to be machined is carefully set up and milling fixture is specially designed for a single component, incorporating jack screws etc. The first operation in milling fixtures requires great skill on the part of the designer.

3. **String or in-line Milling Fixtures:** As the name suggests, this type occupies a considerable length of machine table and holds a number of components in a line or in tandem. The length of the row depends upon the size of the milling machine or its accuracy over a given length of traverse. Unless the machine is provided with a tripping machanism, enabling the table to pass rapidly the blank spaces between the components, care must be exercised in arranging the workpieces close together to reduce the time of air cutting to a minimum. This type of fixture is extensively used for milling forms on the heads of components having a shank. The job is held between hardened and ground vee-blocks which are free to slide in a slot cut in the body of the fixture. Circular pieces without heads can be rigidly constrained only if contacted at three points in the vertical plane, supporting them to be set accurately on one end face in the horizontal plane. If the components concerned are subjected to dimensional variations, as is very often the case, then some form of equalizing or compensating clamping system will almost certainly become necessary. Fig. 6.19.1 shows methods of clamping of such circular workpieces. Such close arrangements avoids air cutting also.

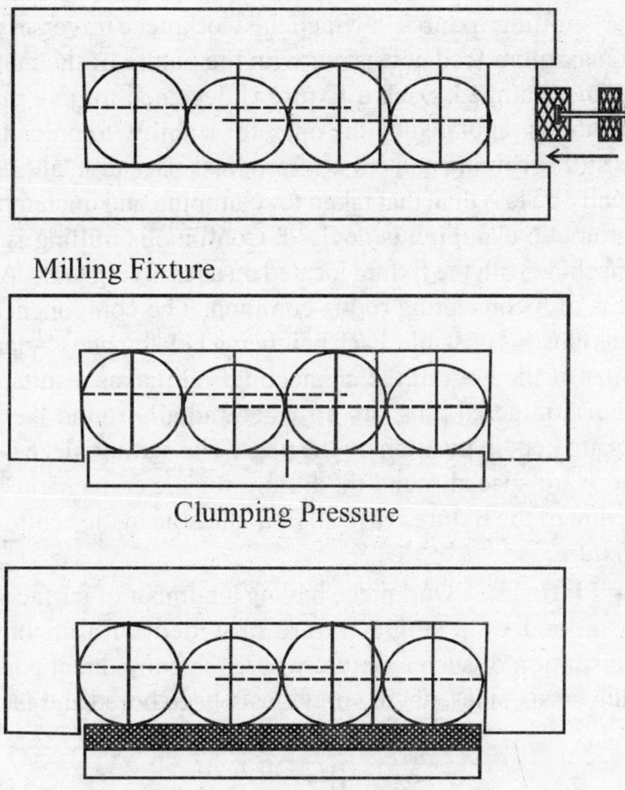

Fig. 6.19.1 (a)

4. **Gang of Straddle Milling Fixtures:** If more than two cutters are used together on the arbor the operation is gang milling or straddle milling. A fixture using gang milling fixtures generally holds several components in a line like line milling fixtures. The heavy cutting load which is generally associated with gang milling makes it necessary to design a very rigid fixture with plenty of metal to absorb the forces set up by cutting tools.
5. **Profile Milling Fixtures:** Profile milling two or three dimensions can be accurately done with relative ease whether the workpiece is flat, uniformly curved, cylindrical, spherical, or irregular in shape, on special profile milling machines. Some of the machines can be used to reduce, enlarge, reverse or insert the shape of the master of a part to master ratio of 1 to 1 or any other ratio within the limits of the machine. The template or master profile is made of hardened steel and the roller maintains close contact with the profile. For short runs the master profile may be made of wood, brass, aluminium, plaster of paris or even cardboard. The movement of the cutter is directly related to the movement of a roller which keeps close contact with the master profile. Thus, the profile of the master is reproduced on the component.

6. **Continuous Rotary Milling fixtures:** The ideal arrangement for milling is with the help of a continuous rotary milling fixtures in which the workpiece traverses past under previously set cutters at the maximum feed consistent with the nature of the material, each one being correctly located and clamped. Such a fixture is designed to give maximum rigidity. The output by this method is regulated by the operator's ability to unload, clean and reload the fixture while it is still revolving and cut is in progress. Because cutting time for this type of fixture would usually be less than that taken for clamping and unclamping by manual means some form of automatic clamping is devised. Continuous milling is best carried out on a vertical spindle machine with the fixture located on a revolving table. A rotary milling fixture for milling process of a connecting rod is common. The component are arranged radially round the fixture as close as possible, each pair being held by one C-clamp. A hole previously drilled in the center of the boss of the connecting rod makes a suitable locating point, for which purpose the shouldered pins, are arranged radially round the fixture. The opposite ends of the pieces are kept in position by the pegs. The setting piece is placed at convenient point and two more are spaced round the fixture for the convenience of the operator. The steel peg in the centre of the fixture is a push fit in the hole in the centre of the revolving table and locates the fixture.
7. **Indexing Milling Fixtures:** A workpiece having a number of surfaces to be milled may be successively positioned by a single fixture provided with an indexing arrangement. Fig. 6.17 is an illustration of such a fixture where the component a hexagonal iron casting requires machining on six sides, having previously been bored and faced.

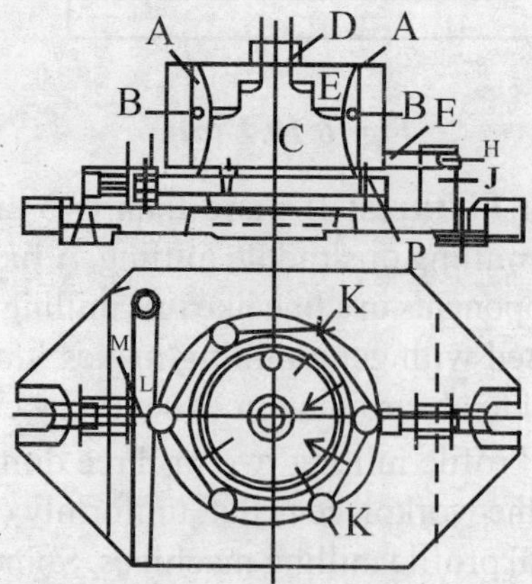

Fig. 6.19.1 (b)

6.19.2 Turning Fixtures

Holding the work pieces for the lathe operations is successfully achieved with the help of numerous types of equipment available, commercially. Such equipment can be classified into chucks, mandrels and collets. To meet particular situations there are further modifications of the three broad classes available. Special chuck jaws can be designed for holding castings and forging for first operations. Expanding mandrels, and pegs find great favour with tool engineers especially where the work affords a machined surface of sufficient accuracy to locate them. When components made from bar on automatic lathes require a second operation they may often be finish machined using a spring collet fitted with an internal stop. However, there still remains a wide variety of components which cannot be effectively held in the above mentioned conventional work holding devices or equipment. Such components require the design of turning fixtures which can be mounted on face plates with the help of dowels and screws. The workpieces are then located and clamped on these turning fixtures for further operations, eliminating the necessity of costly setting.

REVIEW QUESTIONS

1. Define a jig and a fixture, clearly establishing the difference between the two.
2. What are the reasons for using jigs and fixtures?
3. What are the fundamental principles of jig and fixture design? Why a drill jig should have four legs, no more and no less?
4. Classify the drilling jigs and make a sketch of each class. How does a template jig differ from a plate jig?
5. What are the principles of location of drilling jigs? Describe the degrees of freedom of workpiece located in space. Draw a simple sketch to show the 3-2-1 locating principle.
6. List the kind of locators commonly used and explain each with the help of a sketch.
7. What is the function of a clamp in a tool? State the requirements of a good clamping system.
8. With the help of sketches list various clamping devices used on jigs and fixtures.
9. What are the essential elements of a jig and a fixture for milling? Explain the functions of each element with the help of sketches. What are materials and modes of construction of each element?
10 Classify the bushes used in drilling jigs. State where each kind of bush is used. Why must the inner liner of renewable bushing be clamped?
11. What are the various types of milling fixture in use ? Explain each type which an appropriate sketch. What is the difference between an indexing fixture and a continuous rotary fixture?
12. What is an indexing jig? What are the various kinds of indexing devices commonly used?
13. Jigs and fixtures can be produced in many ways. Discuss the merits of each method with reference to the type of production.

Index

A

B

C

G

H

I

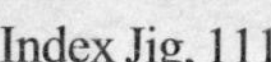

J

L

M

N

O

P

R

S

T

V

W